THE DANCING BEAR

THE
DANCING
BEAR

My Eighteen Years in the
Trenches of the AFL and NFL

RON McDOLE with **ROB MORRIS**

Foreword by GEORGE FLINT

UNIVERSITY OF NEBRASKA PRESS | LINCOLN & LONDON

Library of Congress Cataloging-in-Publication Data

Names: McDole, Ron, author. | Morris, Rob, 1959–, author.
Title: The dancing bear: my eighteen years in the trenches of
the AFL and NFL / Ron McDole with Rob Morris; foreword by
George Flint.
Description: Lincoln: University of Nebraska Press, [2018] |
Includes index.
Identifiers: LCCN 2018009200
ISBN 9781496212610 (cloth: alk. paper)
ISBN 9781496212627 (epub)
ISBN 9781496212634 (mobi)
ISBN 9781496212641 (pdf)
Subjects: LCSH: McDole, Ron. | Football players—United
States—Biography. |
Defensive backs (Football)—United States—Biography. |
National Football
League—History—20th century. | American Football
League—History—20th century.
Classification: lcc gv939.M2995 A3 2018 | ddc 796.332092
[B]—dc23 lc record available at https://urldefense
.proofpoint.com/v2/url?u=https-3a__lccn.loc.gov
_2018009200&d=Dwifag&c=Cu5g146wZdoqVuKptnsyhefx
_rg6kWhlklf8Eft-wwo&r=Qxk-cj_QrVzF1u7b7vxqTw&m
=nhiiciB1Y7qrusygtudjqQ3Ofv_hX0Tle5ahlZhb24E&s=
wz8FgSolofnoBgR6HmT_xzdsuj-hxrxj3OjhebmluXw&e

Set in Lyon Text by Mikala R. Kolander.

There have been so many special people—players, fans, and family—who have been on the journey with me throughout the years and to this day. I would like to dedicate this book to:

Hilton Murphy, my first football coach, who started my interest and taught me how to play football way back in Toledo.

My family, for always believing in me and supporting me—especially Chuck McDole, my brother, an outstanding athlete in his own right who encouraged and helped me to become a great athlete.

Ralph C. Wilson, for hiring me as a Buffalo Bill, giving me the chance to continue my career in football when I thought it was over and allowing me the opportunity to then advance my career with the Washington Redskins.

Lou Saban and George Allen, who were in my opinion the best coaches I played for. They believed in me and my ability to be a part of the team.

Finally, to ALL my teammates from my twenty-five years in football, from high school, college, and professional teams.

—RON MCDOLE

In memory of Paula McDole

—ROB MORRIS

Contents

Foreword

GEORGE FLINT

I first met my good friend Ron McDole in 1963, when he came to the Buffalo Bills in a trade. I'd come to Buffalo in 1962 as a guard out of Arizona State, and then struggled my ass off and made the team in 1962. In 1963, I was struggling again in training camp when Ron showed up. I was one of the smallest guards in the league in 1962, at 6 feet 4 inches and 225, and the Bills were looking for somebody bigger, stronger, and uglier than I was. They'd picked up some high draft picks in the 260–270-pound range. These were guys who not only outweighed me by 50 pounds but could run like deer as well.

Ron showed up to camp after being cut from his previous team, and just by chance, they put Ron and me together as roommates in training camp. Ron became my roommate for the next three years on road trips, until I was traded in 1965 to Oakland. We've remained close friends ever since, even though I live in Flagstaff and he lives in Virginia and neither one of us is too excited about flying.

I got cut in training camp in 1963, but sometimes, decisions about whom to cut are made before training camp begins. I showed up to training camp in 1963 a little heavier and a little stronger, and after they cut me, they paid off the draft picks and hired me back again. So, Ron and I became roommates for the 1963 season as well.

Neither of us made very much money. I think I signed for

$8,500 and Ron was close to that. Hell, in those days, there were Pro Bowl players who made only around $11,000 a year.

Rooming with Ron at training camp was an experience. We had two-a-day practices at camp. We'd have a session in the morning and then a break for lunch and a short rest and another session in the afternoon. After lunch, I would always just want to crap out and rest and here was Ron screwing around and talking and putting on a show, doing strange things like swordfighting and such, and I had to say, "Damn it, Ron! Knock this shit off! If you can't, I'm gonna have to get another roommate!" I had to threaten this every so often, to calm him down so I could get my rest.

Ron had unlimited energy. He'd always want to do stuff after lunch on two-a-days at camp when I wanted to take a nap. And he always had extra energy on the field, too. At the end of a quarter during a football game, when teams changed goal lines, sometimes the ball would have to be moved thirty or forty yards from one end of the field to the other. Ron would run down to the new spot as fast as he could and then wait for all the other guys to stroll up. It was like, "Who is this fat guy who is showing up all the rest of the guys on both teams!?"

The second year we were teammates, Ron called me and asked me whether I could pick him up to take him to training camp. So I drove from where I lived in Arizona up to Toledo, where he was living, and we drove to Erie, Pennsylvania. I was originally from Pennsylvania, and we stopped to visit my grandparents. A lot of us were nervous that year, because there was a threat from the coaching staff that we'd have to show up to camp able to run a mile in full gear. If we couldn't, then we'd have to keep running it till we could. Ron and I went over to the high school track and decided to try to run four laps, which is a mile, to make sure we could do it. We started off, and pretty soon Ron was way ahead of me, and after I'd run about three laps I said, "Oh, screw it! I can suck it up and do this in camp when the pressure is on me. No need to do it right now!" Ron went on and finished his fourth lap. "Where the hell were you?" he asked me when he finished.

"I can do it," I told him. "But I'm going to wait and do it when it counts, for the coaches at training camp!" So, here's Ron, who weighed between 300 and 310 pounds, and he's out there running the mile no problem. The guy was fast, and he was relentless.

One Halloween, at the Bills' Halloween party, Ron dressed up as a ballerina. And he danced a ballet routine for us. He was very graceful. He was a good dancer. Of course, it was very hard for me to appreciate it fully. It took away from his dancing a little bit the way he looked in a tutu.

What makes Ron such a good friend is the fact that the guy will do anything for you. From the moment we started rooming together, we just clicked. He was always trying to negotiate with me, like friends do. "It's your turn to go get the beer!" but it was always lighthearted.

After I retired, Ron kept playing. I went into business. Sometimes I'd call him up and say, "I need to float some money." This was back when you could do that because checks traveled slowly. We'd float checks every so often and occasionally we'd screw it up. But it was all about helping each other.

What makes Ron one of the greats of the game is that he understands the game so well. He is a very, very smart player. He can recognize offenses, and he recognizes the individual offensive player whom he's up against. He can read a lineman by how that lineman is set, and how he's leaning. Also, Ron has amazing hearing. I wouldn't be surprised if he could hear what was being said in the offensive huddle. We'd go out to dinner and he could tell you what was being said a few tables away. The thing that fools some people is that he's such a fun-loving guy that some people didn't take him seriously—until they saw him play. Ron played hard. His pursuit was amazing. He'd chase a runner clear on the other side of the field. It was like he could time his pursuit and gauge the speed of the runner and his own speed and know exactly what angle he needed to make the tackle.

Ron would wake up early in the morning, around 5:00 a.m. at training camp. Everybody else would be fast asleep. I liked to sleep as late as possible. He would get up and sit on the side of his bed and look at me as I lay in the other bed. He was waiting for me to wake up so he'd have somebody to talk to. I'd pretend to be asleep. Then he'd start humming to himself to try to wake me up. I'd roll over. He kept at it. Finally, I'd say, "Oh, screw it!" and I'd get up. Other times, he'd take his chair and go sit in the hallway, waiting for somebody to come by to talk to. At 5:00 a.m., there wasn't anybody.

Why did I put up with it? Why did I put up with his sorry ass? Well, sometimes you just have to put up with people if you really like them.

Preface

ROB MORRIS

Isaac Newton wrote in 1676 that modern men are like dwarves perched on the shoulders of giants. The heights we attain, he said, are only partly the result of our own feeble efforts. We reach these heights because of the sweat and sacrifice of those who came before us. Today's game owes a debt to men whose names are largely forgotten, men who suited up in cramped locker rooms, played in derelict stadiums, and practiced behind motels and in city parks. They played in football's Golden Age—the sixties and seventies. Today, these men are pushing eighty years, at least the ones not sent to an early grave by the game's inherent brutality. Time is running out to hear their stories, to listen to yesterday's giants.

Ron McDole, better known as "The Dancing Bear," waltzed through two decades of pro football on his quick feet and lumbering frame, his ever-present pot-belly tricking less savvy opponents into underestimating the cat-like agility that allowed him to make 13 career interceptions—the most ever by a defensive lineman. Younger players may have looked at the old-school two-bar helmet and thought him antiquated—until he knocked them on their ass. Behind the generously padded exterior and the retro helmet, Ron McDole was a tremendous athlete, admired by teammates and opponents alike, as well as a thinker and logician who could figure out exactly what was going to happen on the field and how he needed to react. Lucky for us, Ron is a natural storyteller blessed with the gift of gab, and in this book, he takes us back to a simpler time when football was as much a game as a business, played by men who loved it so much they didn't mind that they never got rich doing it.

Ron may not be a household name to the casual football fan. But go back and ask the players who played with and against him, and they all have a story of his skill, his wit, or both. They will also tell you Ron is one of the greatest defensive ends to ever play the game. Joe Namath, with whom he partied by night and then harried mercilessly on game day, called me not once but twice to espouse his love and respect for his old friend and nemesis. In a summer of phone calls, player after player told not only of Ron's great skill but also of his sense of fun, his love of jokes, and his skill for spinning a tale out of a mere nothing. To a man, they all respected Ron. Even more importantly, he is universally loved.

Ron's playing career was long. He played from 1961 until 1979. He played more games at defensive end in his career—254—than did any players except Jim Marshall (282) and Bruce Smith (279). Blessed with a work ethic learned in working-class Toledo, Ohio, Ron rarely missed a game. He was one-fourth of one of the greatest defensive lines to ever stride onto the turf—a line that did not allow a single rushing touchdown for a pro record *seventeen* games and yet is virtually forgotten today. Because he played in an era less obsessed with statistics, there is no reliable data on how many sacks, tackles, or blocked field goals or punts Ron amassed, but anyone who was there will tell you it was a hell of a lot.

Ron evolved as a player over the years, incorporating an encyclopedic knowledge of his position and of the actions of his opponents into the edge he needed to keep his job against the young bucks intent on stealing it every year at training camp. When he finally retired at thirty-eight, he'd already been offered a contract by the New York Giants that would have had him playing at forty!

Ron's career runs parallel to many of the great events of the sixties and seventies, from the heady days of postwar prosperity, suburbs, time-saving appliances, and credit cards, to a time of war, economic uncertainty, and political tumult.

Ron also played half his career in one of the pro game's greatest experiments—the exciting new American Football League. Its eight original teams played a free-wheeling, swashbuckling style of football that changed the pro game forever.

Later, in an era whose slogan was "Don't Trust Anyone over Thirty," Ron became part of Redskins coach George Allen's bold idea to build a team based not on youth but on experience, resulting in the "Over-the-Hill Gang," which in 1972 ended the season one game away from the NFL Championship.

Ron showed up every season, gave everything he had on the football field, made a decent living, raised a family, and played at a high level for more years than did almost any other player in history. He never got a fat paycheck. He worked a second job. He played to make a living and because he loved the game.

As the old-school players age, they face new adversaries, including the debilitating effects of brain injury. In 2013, the NFL agreed to pay out $765 million (since raised to almost a billion) to settle a concussion suit filed by forty-five hundred former players on behalf of eighteen thousand retired NFL players. The NFL agreed to compensate affected players, pay for their medical care, and underwrite research into concussions and other TBI. But many feel it won't do enough to protect the very men who made the modern game possible, and who are not as well off financially.

It has been an honor to help Ron write this book. Except where noted, all words are his. So, sit back, put your feet up, and prepare to be taken back to a different time.

Finally, Ron and I would like to thank a few individuals for their kind assistance in writing this book. First and foremost, thanks to Buffalo Bills historian Jeffrey Miller, who proofread the manuscript not once but twice and made sure the Bills history was correct. Second, thank you to Ron's daughter Tammy McDole, who came up with the idea for the book and facilitated its creation. A posthumous thank-you to Ron's wife Paula McDole, and to Ron's wife Toni McDole. Thanks to all the players who shared stories. And finally, my thanks to Ron, for all he has done for football and all he has done to be a genuinely good human being.

Acknowledgments

The authors wish to acknowledge all the players, trainers, equipment managers, and others who were interviewed for this book. From the Buffalo Bills: Ed "Abe" Abramoski, Jim Dunaway, George Flint, Howard Kindig, Ed Rutkowski, Billy Shaw, and Mike Stratton. From the AFL New York Jets: Joe Namath and Frank Ramos. From the Washington Redskins: Mike Bass, Mike Bragg, Larry Brown, Bill Brundige, Dave Butz, Pat Fischer, Ted Fritsch Jr., Chris Hanburger, Ken Houston, Roy Jefferson, Sonny Jurgensen, Bill Kilmer, Tommy McVean, Brig Owens, Myron Pottios, George Starke, and Diron Talbert. Family members of players include Tommy Sestak (son of Tom Sestak), and Ron's own family members: Paula McDole, Antoinette McDole, Tammy McDole, Taz McDole, Tracey McDole. Thanks also to Michael Faley, for sharing his memories of the joy of being a young Buffalo Bills fan in the sixties. Thanks to: Buffalo Bills historian Jeffrey Miller, for reading the manuscript not once, but twice, during its development; Sam Hobbs, for reading the manuscript; Bills photographer Robert L. Smith's family, for the use of his images; Jerry Olsen, executive director of the Alumni of the Washington Redskins; Tammy McDole, for doing all the photo research; and the staff at Timber Ridge School, for their interviews about Ron's philanthropy. Also thanks to our agents, Sam Dorrance and Judy Coppage, and Rob Taylor, Ann Baker, and the staff at the University of Nebraska Press.

THE DANCING BEAR

1
Early Life

I was born in southern Ohio, in a place called Longbottom, which is very close to a town called Chester. I was born in a manger. Literally. My mom was out milking the cows and all of a sudden, here I came! My first name is really Roland. Roland Owen McDole. I was named after the doctor who delivered me. I was born September 9, 1939 (that is, 9/9/39), and I weighed nine pounds, nine ounces. My mother, Ruth, always told me that after that, her favorite number was *not* nine! My dad, Bert, was a farmer until we moved to Toledo, Ohio, when I was six, when Dad took a job with a steel company.

We had a big family and we didn't have a lot of money. Neither of my parents finished high school. My dad worked hard, and my mom, a strict Southern Baptist who took care of all of us, did not smoke or drink. Her children included my oldest brother, Charles (Chuck), then me, then Janice, followed by three more: Jackie, Richard, and Debbie. Charles was a baseball player, five years older than me. That's an awkward age spread, because we were just far enough apart that he regarded me as a pain in the ass. Occasionally, I reinforced that belief.

Neither of my parents had a driver's license. Finally, my older brother, Chuck, got one, and then he bought a blue 1953 Chevy. I talked Mom into buying a new green and white 1956 Chevy Bel Air, with the promise that I would teach her how to drive. She insisted I had to have a job, and she got me one with Red Wells restaurant, because I had to pay half the car payment each month.

I worked as a busboy at Red Wells Roast Beef, which was in a bowling alley. My job was to help wash dishes and clean tables, and I was allowed one free meal per shift. After I had worked there for a few weeks, Mr. Wells came to me and told me I was doing a good job and working hard. He raised my hourly wage from fifty cents to a buck-fifty, but only on the condition that I did not eat at work anymore. I guess eating a whole pie for dessert was excessive.

One year, Charles and his friends were lighting off fireworks when the police showed up. "There's been a report that somebody was lighting off fireworks," the policeman told me. "Any chance it was you?"

"No," I said, "but my brother was," and after I pointed at a house up the street that they were in, I took off and hid somewhere where my brother and his friends could not see me. When the policeman got up there, those boys were stuffing all kinds of explosives down the toilet, under the couch, wherever. It was like a drug raid. My parents were gone at the time, and my brother didn't want them finding out, so he couldn't retaliate against me. But the other guys jumped me later.

My first love was baseball. Baseball was much more popular than football in those days, and I started playing in the Knothole League, like today's Little League. My brother Charles was a great player who ended up playing Minor League pro ball with the Toledo Mud Hens. He finally quit baseball because he hated the long bus rides and thought that trying to make the big leagues was too much of a long shot, too big of a gamble. Charles had gotten married and had two young sons, and he needed a steady job. So instead of taking a chance and possibly becoming a professional baseball player, he decided to stay at home and continue working as a tool- and-die maker.

I became a catcher because my brother was a pitcher. That way he would have somebody to throw to. Nobody wanted to play catcher anyway, because nobody wanted to get whacked with a ball or a bat or what-have-you. Later, after I got to high school, I had an excellent coach by the name of Norm Kies. He was a former professional baseball player who'd played on the New York Yankees. He'd been hit in the eye by a foul ball and had to retire, so he became a physical education teacher. It was a real plus to have a baseball coach who was an ex–big leaguer, because he knew what had to be done to make it to the big leagues. Norm was also my academic advisor, and he was an important mentor to me in high school.

We'd always played a little football in the neighborhood, the same kind kids play today. You know, whoever brought the football got to be the quarterback. We played in an alley, gravel and black top. The quarterback would run the show. In the huddle, it would just be, "You, Billy, go down to that green car and turn left. And you, Johnny, go as far as you can straight down the alley and make the catch. And the rest of you guys, block!" For years, I thought "the rest of you guys, block" was a position. That was *my* position.

I was big but not super-big, and somebody asked me, "Why don't you play on the football team?" I liked baseball much better, but I decided to give football a try. I played junior high football in Toledo, in what was called the West Toledo Athletic League. The teams were sponsored and were loosely affiliated with the nearest school. There were eight junior high teams in the league. The games were played Saturday nights under the lights, and the league was run by the parents. We had to buy our own uniforms. Nothing fancy. That was my initiation to football. I played from sixth grade on and that was my first time playing football. I didn't even know the rules. All I knew were alley rules.

All of us neighborhood kids were now sent off to different high schools. Due to the location of my house I was sent to Thomas A. DeVillbis High School. DeVillbis was in a wealthy section of Toledo. We were considered from the rough side of town and DeVillbis was a kind of elite, rich school. The other schools called us "the cake eaters."

DeVillbis was also an all-white school. I didn't know any black people till I started playing college football at Nebraska. I made the high school football team as a sophomore and made the baseball team as well. There was a problem on the baseball team, though, because I'd always been a catcher and the best guy on the high school team was a catcher. I tried pitching a little bit, and then ended up at first base. I've always had to play in an active position in any sport. I love being involved in every play. I could never stand out in the outfield and wait for a ball to come my way.

When I was a senior, we made the playoffs in baseball and went to the semifinals. We showed up for the semifinal game in a little farm town and assumed we would be playing some rag-tag, cow-town team. Sure enough, when we showed up in this little town, we saw a bunch of guys running a raggedy drill. They looked terrible. We figured we'd slaughter them. As we warmed up for our victory, we noticed that there was a track meet being held on the track next to the baseball field. Soon, the track meet got over, and this track kid came over in his track uniform and put on a baseball uniform. That kid went out to the mound and mowed us down. I think we got one hit. He threw the ball about one hundred miles per hour!

As a senior playing football, I was moved from the line to fullback. I had to lose some weight, and got down from 250–270 to 210–220. It was now up to me to run over the top of all my opponents, which was a welcome change.

My goal after graduation originally was to be a tool- and-die maker like my dad and older brother. Toledo made a lot of parts for the Detroit auto industry. But as it got time for college, I had other things to consider. First, I had a girlfriend, Paula, who had transferred from an all-girls Catholic school, and we were thinking about getting married. Her parents expected her to go to college, and she'd won a full-ride diving scholarship to Purdue, and I think Paula kind of expected me to go to college, too.

We wanted to get married out of high school, but her father

was against it. As a competitive diver, Paula traveled all over the country and had gotten a scholarship to Purdue to dive with the top coach in the country. She was training for the Olympics and competed internationally, too. Her dad did not want her to give up her scholarship. He was against us getting married and did not want us to be together and at the same college.

When it came time for college, quite a few colleges offered me scholarships. I had offers from Ohio State, Kent State, Purdue, Nebraska, and others. I still wasn't planning on going, though. Then, my baseball coach and high school advisor, Norm Kies, gave me some life-changing advice. Coach Kies told me that Detroit was interested in signing me for the Minor Leagues. He said, "I advise you to go to college and go to Nebraska. Take the football scholarship for football and try out for the college baseball team and it will be like playing in the Minor Leagues."

Kies told me that he was friends with Tony Sharp, the baseball coach at Nebraska. They were teammates together in the pros. Norm said he'd call Tony and that he was sure Tony would be happy to get a baseball player on a football scholarship, and I'd have the advantage of working with a former professional player. Playing for Tony would be the equivalent of playing in the Minor Leagues. It would be a tremendous opportunity. So, the main reason I chose Nebraska was because of baseball, and because of Tony Sharp. I also ultimately chose Nebraska because I wanted to be an industrial arts teacher, and Nebraska was one of the few schools with a good industrial arts degree. I went off to Nebraska and Paula went off to Purdue to train for the Pan America Games. I was the first one in the McDole family to go to college.

We kept in touch, and the last year of school we decided that we wanted to get married. Paula had transferred to Ohio State by that time. Her parents were not happy about it and it was a battle; they said if we got married we were going to have to do it on our own, and they didn't even come to the wedding. (We got married twice, once by the justice of the peace and once in the church on the campus of the University of Nebraska, Lincoln.)

She needed one class to finish her degree, which she took at Nebraska, and we had our honeymoon during the bowl games that I was playing in (Blue-Gray, Senior Bowl).

Realistically, though she still competed and dove, Paula gave up her dream to dive in the Olympics for my career. She gave it up to support me and raise our family. I was always amazed that she did that for me, because she was very successful as a diver; she was good enough to medal in the Olympics. She said that diving and winning a medal was just one thing, where me playing ball could be a career and we could make money.

Paula always stepped up and supported me and my career. She taught school in Buffalo for underprivileged and special needs kids. She had to work, because at that time I made only around $9,000 a year playing football, and we had a family to support.

She was always helpful in getting my furniture company going (Ron McDole Library Furniture). She worked well with the dealers and sales, and later she went on to become an appraiser.

She also took care of the kids, moving the family back and forth once I got traded to Washington. She could have left at any time, but she hung in there and supported me and kept working even when she did not have to. And I always knew that she would handle everything while I was gone. Paula gave up everything to make it all work from the beginning, and I have always been amazed and grateful for that.

2
The University of Nebraska

Prior to my arrival at Nebraska, the Huskers struggled a bit in the fifties, going through six head coaches. In 1956, Coach Bill Glassford was replaced by Bill Jennings, who would be my coach throughout my Nebraska playing career.

When I showed up in 1957, the university had eight thousand students. It was a beautiful campus, with plenty to do, from gathering around a homecoming bonfire to going to dances. But the best entertainment of all happened on game day, when it seemed like all Nebraska turned out in red to cheer on the home-team Cornhuskers.

I became part of the great Nebraska football-building program, pretty much a complete revamping. The first year I was there, we won only one game. The great team in the conference in those days was Oklahoma. Coach Bud Wilkinson's Sooners hadn't been beaten in the Big Eight Conference in thirteen years.

To build up its football program, Nebraska dumped in tons of money. Instead of giving football scholarships, they went out and recruited academically talented athletes and gave them academic scholarships, some of which were privately funded. This meant there was no limit to the number of scholarships. They recruited athletes with high grades from all over the country. That was the beginning of the tradition. Even today, if you look at the average grades of the Nebraska football team, they're very high. The O-line still averages an A-minus.

Three of the guys who played at Nebraska with me ended up having long professional football careers. Even though we four played together on the same team, we didn't accomplish much other than winning a couple of big games. However, we all went on to long careers and over eighty-five combined years in the pros.

Of the four of us, I was the only non–Nebraska native. The first Husker teammate who ended up having a long career in the NFL was center Mick Tingelhoff. Mick and his wife, Phyliss, lived above us in the same duplex, and his daughter Terri was born three days after our daughter Tammy. Mick didn't start until his senior year, but he ended up being co-captain on that team, earning himself a spot in the Senior Bowl and the All-American Bowl. He was drafted by Minnesota, and I was with him in Minnesota for about two weeks after I'd been cut by Houston and before I went to Buffalo. Mick played center. He played his entire seventeen-year career at Minnesota, where he became a great player. He was inducted into the Hall of Fame in 2015, an honor he richly deserved. Ironically, I thought that of the three of us from Nebraska, Pat Fischer would be the first one inducted into the Hall if any of us were going to go.

Monte Kiffin has coached for at least fifty years in college and in the NFL. He was one of our offensive tackles at Nebraska. The only thing we really did when we all played together for Nebraska was, we beat Oklahoma at a time when Oklahoma dominated everything in the late fifties. When we beat them for the first time in thirteen years in the conference, it was a big deal—the university gave the whole campus the day off. Monte went on to play professionally in 1966 with both the Toronto Rifles and the Brooklyn Dodgers of the CFL. Monte then went on to a long and successful coaching career at the college and pro level ever since, and is considered by many to be the top defensive coordinator in the history of modern football. His coached defenses have finished in the NFL top ten in points allowed and yards allowed ten times. Monte coached on the Cowboys, the Tampa Bay Buccaneers (where he invented the Tampa Cover 2 defense), and in

March 2016 he signed a contract as a defensive assistant with the Jacksonville Jaguars.

The third, Pat Fischer, became one of my closest friends. He still is, to this day. Pat Fischer's and my careers run parallel a lot of the time in a way that is uncanny. Pat and I have been close for nearly sixty years now. He's got some memory issues, but we still have a great time when the two of us get together. As I wrote this book, we met and talked at length about our parallel careers, which I'm including a description of here as an appendix.

Ironically, I started out at Nebraska as a tight end. Mostly a blocking tight end. In one game, against Iowa State, I caught the winning touchdown near the end of the game. We won that one, 7–6. Eventually, they switched me to the line.

We never had a winning season while I was at Nebraska. Our coach, Bill Jennings, was only so-so. He didn't have the greatest coaching staff, he had only thirty players, and our first year we won one game. By the time I left, we might have gotten up to four or five wins in a season. Nebraska was just beginning to build a great football program. We were there at the beginning.

In the spring my freshman year, I also tried out for the Nebraska baseball team and made the team with no problem. However, the athletic department would not let me miss spring football practice to play baseball. Over the years, I got better at football. Two teammates of mine, Pat Fischer and Don Fricke, as well as myself, were tri-captains, and a captain could not miss practice. I thought after the end of my senior year playing football I could go play baseball. However, I was now considered a professional athlete because I'd played in the Senior Bowl, which is coached by the NFL, so I lost my eligibility to play baseball.

I played both ways at Nebraska. I still hold the record for being in the game on nearly every play one season. Somebody told me that somebody figured out that I played 1,074 out of a possible 1,200 minutes that year.

It wasn't without occasional problems. In one game, they used some chemical to line the field that mixed with the dye in our uniforms. I got a lot of it inside my pants and it burned my butt really, really badly. They thought I'd need skin grafts. But we just took some elastic pants, kind of like modern Under Armour, and filled them with gel, to create a ball joint, and in a week or two I was almost back to normal.

I also got mono and missed a lot of school. I had to drop some courses and take incompletes, and that made me delinquent as far as my scholarship. To stay current, I took a class on teaching driver's ed that summer. I figured since I was going to be a teacher anyway, I might as well learn how to teach kids to drive.

If you stayed at the university in the summertime, which I did, you had the option of staying at the firehouse. Sliding down the pole was fun, but getting up every time the firemen got called to a fire in Lincoln, Nebraska, was not so much fun—and you didn't get to ride on the fire truck. Instead, I roomed with the Rhodes family. They were big supporters of Nebraska athletics and were very good to me. I would work odd jobs, like babysitting their kids, so that I could earn a little money.

One time, when I got hurt, Mr. Rhodes told me, "Stay at our house, get your credits. I don't give a damn if you ever play another game for the University of Nebraska. In fact, I'll pay for your education if I have to." That's just what kind of guy he was. I made my son Tracey's middle name Rhodes.

Paula switched from Purdue to Nebraska when I was a senior, and we got married in Council Bluffs, Iowa, because Iowa didn't have a waiting period for a marriage license. Paula had to take one course to graduate from Nebraska. We had our official wedding in Lincoln, Nebraska, and our honeymoon at the Blue-Gray Bowl in Montgomery, Alabama.

Life was becoming more complicated. I was a college student, I was now married, and I was trying not only to finish up my degree but also to support my family. Our daughter Tammy was born in 1961, so I added parent to my responsibilities. My teammate Mick Tingelhoff, future Viking and Hall of Famer, was also married with a baby, and he used to come over and we'd babysit our kids while our wives went to bridge club. We'd experiment with making different mixed drinks, using stuff like chocolate, bananas, and vodka, and we drank it. Our palates were not highly developed in those days.

Scholarship athletes could not work when school was in session, so we were always hurting for money. We had most of our expenses paid for, and received a fifteen-dollar laundry fee. But as a married student, I needed more money than most college students did, and they let the married students work a little to make some extra money. This led to some interesting jobs during breaks and summer vacation.

One year, I got a job with the Stroh's Beer Company. My job was to ride with a veteran route driver and deliver beer to Lincoln-area bars. My job was to load and unload the beer. Lincoln was a dry city at the time. Only beer was legal, and then only if you were twenty-one.

I'd unload the truck, tap the kegs in the basement, and then talk to the people a bit. I hated tapping kegs, because the basements of these bars were always filled with spiders and I'm afraid of spiders. I not only hate spiders—I hate all bugs and snakes, all of them. But it was part of the job. After I'd tapped the kegs, I couldn't get out of the bars because people were all fabulous Nebraska fans, so they all knew me, and they would grab me to have a beer with them and talk about what we were going to do on the field in the upcoming game. I'd have to have a beer with fans at each stop!

Eventually I asked the driver whether we could drink some of the beer on the truck. "Only if we have breakage," he said. Ten minutes later, he hit the brakes hard, and there was a big crash in the back, and then my driver said, "go back and get us some breakage and we'll have a beer." When I got home after some trips, I was so drunk I called Paula to come pick me up. She was pissed off, and that was it for me as a beer delivery guy.

"Ron's having a lot of problems," my supervisor said. "His

wife is on his ass about delivering beer." So he decided to make me a loader. I'd load the truck in Omaha, on a truck going from the factory rather than coming back. When we get there, they give us some beer, right off the shelf, hot as hell. "Are you going to drink that hot beer?" I asked the driver.

"Yeah," he said. "It's good." "Well. Okay. Maybe I'll try it," I said. It really wasn't half bad. I got so shit-faced on that trip that Paula had to come get me again. That was the end of my Stroh's career.

After I got mono I worked at a Russell Stover candy factory. Working at Russell Stover helped me put my weight back on after my mono, plus even a little more weight. One of my jobs was taste-testing their new creation, chocolate-covered grapes. I'm not sure whether they ever put them on the market or not. There were four or five floors at the factory, and they finally moved me to the shipping area, but I still found a way to get food. Eventually, I ate so much candy that they threw me out.

In high school, I'd won awards for industrial arts. We had a great program at my high school, and I decided at that time that I would really like to teach industrial arts at either the junior high or senior high level. My high school always stuck all the kids with behavior problems in industrial arts. My teacher, Mr. Grubbs, came to me while I was in high school and asked me whether I wanted to teach the two o'clock machine shop class for him, to help him out. I did, and it worked out. In fact, I really enjoyed it. That was one of the main reasons I went to Nebraska.

There was a high school on campus at Nebraska, set up to train the teachers. I student-taught there and then taught one year as a shop teacher, and I also taught a section of history. At the time of my student-teaching—which I completed after I played for the Houston Oilers—I pretty much had complete control of what I did in class. The actual teacher just dropped in every so often to supervise. Well, at the same time I was buying old houses and then turning them into apartments to make a little extra money. I'd also bought a little Fiat. Of course, back then you couldn't get Fiat parts in Nebraska, and the brakes went out. So I created a molding class and had my molding class mold some brake parts for my Fiat. Also, since I was fixing up houses, I had my students working on ductwork for the houses. One day, my supervisor popped in while everybody was working on ductwork for the house.

"Why is everybody working on ductwork?" he asked. "It's real-world," I explained. "Then, why is everyone making the same thing? It looks like somebody's house's ductwork."

I also taught one section of American history. I had enjoyed American history in school, and had always paid attention, or at least I thought I had. But teaching it is another thing. I worked very hard on my lesson plans, but I was never more than a day or two ahead of the place I was teaching on any given day. And there was this one little kid in the class, really smart, always reading ahead. I was at most *one* chapter ahead. And he'd always raise his hand. I'd say, "Yes, Jimmy?" "Mr. McDole," he'd ask, "what if Burgoyne had done such and such at the Battle of Such and Such?"

I'd think "Oh, hell," because I hadn't got to that part myself, and all the other kids would snicker. I had an advisor who had taught school, and I went to her with this problem. She had just the solution for me. She said, "The next time Jimmy asks you a question, here's what you do . . . ." The next time Jimmy's hand shot up, I called on him and he asked his question, and I said, "Jimmy, that is a good question. Here's what I want you to do. I want you to go home and research that, and then write a report about what you find out. Then you can present it to the class tomorrow." Well, Jimmy did the report, but I noticed he never asked any more of those questions.

Long story short, I finished up at the University of Nebraska, got my degree, and was all ready to teach the next year if need be. In 1960, there was a new football league, the American Football League, and the AFL decided to hold its college draft before the NFL did. The NFL didn't like it, but there was nothing they could do about it. The AFL draft for graduating 1961 college players was held in the fall of 1960. They did it on November 21 and 22, and they held the first six rounds by telephone. They finished the draft on December 5 and 6, with rounds seven through thirty.

Players weren't too selective about NFL or AFL, so long as the money was right. They also had the option of playing in Canada, where the salaries were good. Back in those days, lots of times professional teams had college coaches on their payrolls, looking out for pro teams on the side, looking for potential talent.

I was drafted in the fourth round by the AFL's Denver Broncos. The Broncos called me up and flew me out to a game. Afterward, we went to a hockey game with the coach, Frank Filchock, who was an ex–NFL player. Filchock had been a star quarterback and halfback for the New York Giants before getting caught up in a game-fixing scandal in the 1946 NFL title game with the Bears. Filchock got kicked out of the NFL and went to Canada and played up there until he started coaching.

Filchock took me to the Broncos locker room after the Broncos game. Half the players were old NFL players who'd jumped over to the AFL. Here they were, sitting around in the locker room watching an NFL game on two televisions and drinking Coors beer. I thought, "Hell, this isn't too bad!" Still, I wanted to hold out for the NFL, so I didn't sign. I think Denver offered me around $10,000 for that first year.

I also had some interest from the Canadian Football League. Winnipeg even sent a scout down, saying they were willing to offer me $14,000 a year.

A month later, the NFL had its draft. Teams had called me ahead of time to see whether I was available. They didn't want to waste a draft choice if I was going to stay in Denver. At this point, I hadn't signed a contract with Denver—I'd only had their offer. The 49ers called me every day. They wanted to draft me as an offensive guard. Both the 49ers and the Rams had been pestering me to death, and I was sure I'd end up on the 49ers,

Cowboys, or Rams. I was playing in one of the college All-Star Games, either the Blue-Gray Game or the Senior Bowl, while the NFL draft was going on. After those games, I was getting lots of phone calls from NFL teams. The draft went late. Paula and I were at a dance the night of the draft, and I finally went up to the motel room about midnight not knowing whether I'd been drafted. When I woke up in the morning, I bought a paper. Before I had a chance to read it, I was paged by the hotel. I went to the phone and it was the Cardinals' defensive coach, Chuck Drulis. "Congrats," he said, "We drafted you last night in the fourth round." I told him I'd be there the next day.

The Cardinals had just moved from Chicago to St. Louis that season. The funny thing about them drafting me is that I had never heard anything from them up to that point. They never even sent me a card. I was shocked that they'd picked me up. I stumbled around thanking him on the phone, saying how happy I'd be to play for them, but in truth I didn't know anything about the Cardinals. Drulis told me he'd be there the following morning, and I said okay. I went back up to my room and Paula asked, "Did you get drafted?" I told her, "Yes, I did." Paula was a big football fan. "What round?" I said, "Either the third or the fourth."

The next day, Drulis showed up. I can't remember whether he took us out to lunch or not. Drulis was the toughest, roughest, foulest-mouthed guy in the world. He started making small talk with me. "How much money do you want?" he asked. "Well," I told him. "Winnipeg offered me $14,000." "Fourteen thousand?!" he said. "Wow! That's great!" I said, "And Denver offered me ten thousand and then some." He said, "Well, I tell ya what. I'll give you $9,000." "I don't know," I said. "I think I can do better than that."

He thought for a minute, then he said. "Okay, I'll give you $9,250. And," he added, "we'll help you buy a brand-new car." I wasn't sure exactly what he meant by *help* me buy a brand-new car. Did that mean they were going to *buy* me a brand-new car? "Or," he said, "we'll just let you go and pick you up later on waivers."

I wanted to play in the NFL. So, I signed for $9,250. When I signed, the Cardinals gave me a baby-blue Pontiac convertible. I was still teaching school, and I really didn't drive it very much. The other players, the single ones, would borrow it because it looked sporty and they'd take it on dates. On one occasion, we were driving in the convertible and we looked back and our daughter Tammy was crawling around on the boot. That was it—we traded it in on a sedan.

Pat Fischer and I didn't know it at the time we signed, but if new players made the Cardinals team, and you were one of the remaining thirty-two guys, you got an extra $500. We both made it, and we both got it in our first paycheck.

In St. Louis, right out of college, Pat Fischer and I didn't know much about the professional game. We didn't really know its rich history. We hadn't even really heard about many of the players, and there were great ones that came before us. On St. Louis, we had Sonny Randle. I learned more about the history of the early league later.

Looking back on that first year, it's interesting to reflect on the draft class of 1961. I was taken as the first pick of the fourth round, number 25 overall. Also in the 1961 AFL draft were the future Hall of Famers Mike Ditka (1), Billy Shaw (2), Herb Adderly (2), and Bob Lilly (2). Drafted after me.

3

A Cardinal, Then an Oiler, Then a Viking

Paula, Tammy, Pat Fischer, and I drove from Nebraska to training camp in Chicago for our rookie season with the Cardinals. I was driving, with Paula in the passenger seat of our little Fiat. Poor Pat Fischer was squeezed into the tiny back seat, which he shared with our daughter Tammy, whom we had in a basket. Tammy had colic and cried all the way to Chicago. Pat did a great job of trying to keep Tammy calmed down. That Fiat was about ready to burst at the seams. When we approached Chicago, Pat Fischer's eyes just kept getting wider and wider. He was a Nebraska boy, and he'd never seen a big city before. He couldn't believe it. He kept saying, "My God, look at these roads!"

Pat was a seventeenth-round draft choice, and he probably wouldn't have been drafted at all except for Ray Prochaska. Prochaska had been a coach at Nebraska and was an offensive line coach on the Cardinals. Prochaska was the one who recommended Pat and me to the Cardinals organization. Pat was a multidimensional player. He could play offense or defense. We all had to play both, but he was an amazing safety. Fisher had an uncanny ability to read a receiver. Just by looking at the receiver, he could usually tell where the receiver was going to go. Pat's only about 5 feet 9 inches and 170, so he had to be very smart to play so many years in the NFL and be so successful. Playing offense in college taught him to think like an offensive player, which really helped while playing as a defensive player. This also helped me during my AFL and NFL career. I intercepted a lot of passes, and the main reason was that I played some offensive end in college (same as a tight end), which helped me to create a feel for catching the ball.

When I reported to the Cardinals, I thought I'd have a starting job. Frank Fuller, the starting defensive tackle from the previous year, had retired. I was the highest-rated rookie in camp. But then Frank Fuller came back, and I was in limbo. We had a couple of other great linemen on St. Louis. There were Don Owens and Luke Owens, two great tackles, huge guys.

The rosters in those days were much smaller—teams carried only thirty-four players. But that year, the Cardinals cut it even more, to thirty-two.

Because the Cardinals had been the old Chicago Cardinals, and had just moved down to St. Louis, our training camp was held north of Chicago, at Lake Forest College. For the first time, I saw some of these big guys, big names, who had been playing for years, guys like John David Crow, who was our halfback, or Sonny Randle—guys that I knew about because I'd casually followed football. There were a lot of older guys on that team who had been around for many years. We had Frank Fuller, and Ed Henke, guys who by that time were in their thirties. And to me, those guys seemed ancient, though I'd laugh about that later in my career as a member of the "Over-the-Hill Gang." We were there to take the older guys' jobs, and we all realized that, but there were still guys who would help you out, like Ed Henke. The camp really wasn't that much different from a college training camp. The last couple of weeks of camp, we moved down to St. Louis, but we didn't have a facility there.

In St. Louis, there was a sort of "hazing" during camp, nothing bad. The older players used to make the rookies sing. At dinner, they would call your name, and when your name was called you had to sing your college fight song, or any song. You never knew when you were going to be called; however, when they called your name you would have to stand up in front of everyone and sing.

Taz Anderson, a rookie from Georgia Tech, was my roommate in camp. I knew we would both be picked to sing eventually. I really did not know the Nebraska fight song, so I was practicing a song that was popular at the time—I don't remember what it was. Sure enough, one day at dinner they called on Taz to sing his fight song, and he gets up and sings the song I had been practicing forever! I thought to myself, "What the *hell*?!"

Of course, they called on me next because we were roommates, I stood up and said, "He stole my song!" The guys said, "Tough! Sing your fight song!" So, I stood there humming the song and filling in the words that I *did* know, which was about four or five. It was embarrassing, and it got me lots of razzing. Thanks, Taz!

In St. Louis, things were disorganized. It was a hectic year, in some ways, and kind of a weird entrance into the National Football League. The team had just moved. The owner, Violet Bidwell, had inherited the team from her late husband, Charles, and she and her St. Louis businessman husband, Walter Wolfner, decided that the Chicago Cardinals couldn't really compete being overshadowed by the Chicago Bears. The NFL approved the team's move to St. Louis, where there would now be two teams with the same name. It wasn't ideal, really. St. Louis didn't have a stadium just for football. We had to play in the baseball stadium, Sportsman's Park, with the infield dirt and everything, and share it with the baseball St. Louis Cardinals. The baseball team didn't let us practice at Sportsman's Park; we were allowed to play games there only on Sundays. For practices, we'd pile onto several buses and drive around until we found a city park that wasn't too busy and we'd practice there. One time, we even practiced in a barn, on a dirt horse ring. While we practiced in that stable, the gosh darn horses all watched us and probably wondered what the hell was going on!

We had several different coaches that year, starting with Chuck Drulis. Drulis had played 72 games, mostly in Chicago, as an offensive guard. He was tough, and he cussed like a sailor—ranting, raging, yelling, cussing you out, and being just generally nasty.

One day in practice he jumped all over me. I was thinking that I did not know what I was doing and feeling a bit down. I walked back to the huddle and Ed Henke said, "Isn't he lovely?" Henke was an old defensive end who'd been playing pro ball since 1949, both in Canada and in the NFL, so he was a real old-timer.

"He is really riding me," I answered. "I'm not sure what I'm doing." Ed told me, "Be happy that he is. If he didn't think you were any good and could learn, he wouldn't spend time yelling at you. He's not going to waste his time on someone he doesn't think can play."

"The best advice I can give you," he continued, "is to do what they say, do it how they want it done, and do your best in practice, even if you know or feel that what they're telling you isn't right. Then, when you're in the game, play what you know."

That was some of the best advice I ever received. I had never looked at it that way before. I learned so much from these guys. Ed was like a father to me. He would hate that I said that.

During the season, Coach Drulis was replaced by Pop Ivy as head coach. Coach Frank "Pop" Ivy was a good guy. He'd been around the game a long time, first as a player and then as a coach. He'd coached in Canada, and he was trying to put in a Canadian-style offense, which has movement toward the line on every snap. Coach Ivy also had good discipline, and he must have liked me, because he asked me to play for him in Houston, too.

I made the team as a defensive end and also played a little guard, but I didn't start. I mostly played special teams. On defense, I played behind a kid named Joe Rabb. Ed Henke was on the other side.

In the opening game, which happened to be against the New York Giants, I was in on the kickoff team on the first play of the game. I was L1, the first guy beside the kicker, and I ran down the field full-speed into a crushing hit. Blood went everywhere! I was wearing my two-bar mask and the hit snapped both bars off the mask. My nose got pushed over to the side. They packed some cotton up my nose and fitted me with a cage helmet, and

I went back in on the very next kickoff. Welcome to the NFL. I played the rest of the game. It was the only time I wore a cage helmet. I do not like a cage helmet, never have. I wore the old double-bar helmet. There was a reason I preferred the double-bar helmet. I like seeing. Because I'd played on the offensive line in college, and occasionally at St. Louis, I'd learned that I really didn't particularly like to get hit. My philosophy was "if you're gonna hit me, I want to see you." I played eighteen years with a double-bar helmet. I think I might have been the only lineman to do that by the end of my career. And I never had any trouble. The cage helmet became very popular during my playing career. Nowadays, players wear all kinds of stuff on their helmets to protect themselves, including plastic shields, and they cover their face and head up because they use their head and face so much when they're blocking.

Pat Fischer and I had that first year together, on the St. Louis Cardinals, in 1961. I went a little higher in the draft than Pat did, but we started out together and we both made the team in 1961. The Cardinals took a real beating that year due to injuries. We lost so many guys during the season. The Cardinals did not know what to do with Fischer because he was so small, about 5 feet 9 inches and 170, but Pat used to just knock the hell out of people. Pat had played quarterback and running back at Nebraska. So, they kept moving him around trying to find just the right place for him. They did the same with me. I was getting pushed from offensive to defensive line and we were both struggling hard to make the team. We made it, but we struggled all through the season. Pat ended up being a corner, and that's where he would play for the rest of his career. Pat was small, but he had a mantra that is still used today by smaller defensive corners and safeties: "Get a leg up and you own him."

The sixties were a time of great change in race relations, and the football world was not immune. Growing up Ohio, I hadn't been exposed to segregation. But that changed when I began playing football at Nebraska. College was the first time many of us were exposed to black players. It was the first time I'd gotten to know a black person, and the first time I had seen racism, and I didn't like it. I never had a problem getting along with anybody. How can you dislike somebody you don't even know? Even though I went to an all-white high school in Toledo, I just never saw people in terms of their color. The first black person I really knew was Clay White, who was my teammate at Nebraska. Clay ended up being a good friend of mine, and we worked on the interstate highway construction in Nebraska, out in the middle of nowhere. There were very few black people in Nebraska, except those who were athletes on the sports teams. The main minority in the state was Native people. I remember one game, at Oklahoma, we sat on a bench that was right up against the seats. Oklahoma had a black player named Prentice Gautt, who ended up playing for Cleveland and the Cards. On a punt, Gautt caught the punt and started running it upfield. After Clay White knocked the shit out of him, some white guy in the stands, right behind me, yells to the officials a very derogatory remark at Clay, involving the "N"-word.

When Pat Fisher and I went to the Cardinals, we never really had much contact with the black players, though they seemed nice. After our first home game, an exhibition game, we had a party in downtown St. Louis, and I noticed there were no black players at the party. Pat and I talked about it because it was so different and strange to us. The next day, I walked over to Ed Henke and asked him about it. "They're not allowed to come here," Ed said.

The next day, at practice, I went over to Luke Owens, the black tackle, a very good guy, and I asked him what he thought about not being able to go to the party.

"Ain't that a bitch?" he said. "We can get beat up with you on the football field, but we're not allowed to party with you. We have a separate party." This was the first racial incident that I had ever run into. Things changed. We made sure that everyone went to the parties. Some of the veteran players got behind it and said that the whole team should celebrate together.

We went to Jacksonville, Florida, to play Pittsburgh in the Gator Bowl. We landed in Jacksonville and got off the plane. There were two cars down on the tarmac for the black guys. Jimmy Hill, one of our black players, and another black player were given the car keys and the black players got into the cars and drove away. They weren't allowed to stay at our hotel, which is also where we had our meetings. We didn't see our black teammates again until we showed up at the stadium for the game. I asked, "Why can't the black players even come to the meetings?" That's just the way it was done, they explained. I thought this was very strange, and it really bothered me. I remembered that at the Blue-Gray game back in 1961, the black fans had to sit in the end zone. That also really bothered me.

It happened again the next year when we went to Florida for a game. My black teammates stayed somewhere else and we saw them at game time. I love everybody on Sunday. I don't care if you're black, white, yellow, or green. We all have to get along on Sunday.

During my rookie season, the communist East German government, concerned about the brain drain to the west, put up the Berlin Wall, effectively preventing access between the communist East and the democratic West. Tensions escalated between President John F. Kennedy and Soviet leader Nikita Khrushchev. NFL players had signed up for a controlled military group. Since I was married, and had a child, I was exempt. My Nebraska teammate Pat Fisher was also exempt because of college. But amazingly, when the Berlin Crisis hit, many NFL guys got called up to the Controlled Military Group, including Taz Anderson, our center, Bob DeMarco, one of our tackles, Ernie McMillan, and some others. Ernie McMillan (who was a rookie that year) ended up working on helicopters. He got out by telling the Cardinals he'd sign a new contract if they got him out, and they did.

In my time with the Cardinals, I was under so much stress, so much pressure, to make the team. I had a wife and now two kids, as our son Taz had been born. I didn't have my teaching degree yet. I started to get migraines. My rookie year, the Cardinals had me playing offensive tackle, which I wasn't too thrilled about. I didn't like blocking and I didn't like head slaps. If you get migraines, getting slapped on the side of your helmet every play is not helpful.

The stress is probably what triggered the migraines. The owners of the Cardinals when I was drafted were the Bidwells. The Bidwells had two sons, Stormy and Billy. Stormy was okay, but Billy was really a nasty guy. Mr. Bidwell died and his ex-wife inherited the team. She married a guy named Mr. Wolfner. She owned the team; however, Mr. Wolfner ran it. It was confusing, because Mr. Wolfner was always around and she was never around. This was the first year that they had owned the team after moving from Chicago. After the end of my first season, Mrs. Wolfner passed away in Florida.

Then it became a huge legal mess as to who owned the ballclub. Wolfner sued saying it was his ballclub, while the kids were suing because they said it was their ballclub, and it was very hectic. I signed a contract for my second year with Stormy at an exhibition game in Omaha for the next year. The lawsuit went on forever. When the dust settled, it was decided that the Bidwells owned the club. They settled the suit, and Stormy took the racetracks and Billy took the Cardinals.

That year, I played in fourteen games, mostly on special teams. Pat Fischer returned kicks and caught a pass.

When I showed up to camp the next year, Billy called me into the office and said the contract that I signed with Stormy was no longer valid and I was cut. I had a $500 advance. It wasn't a bonus, but an advance, and Billy said he wanted it back.

I could have fought my dismissal on grounds of the broken contract, but at that time I just wanted out of there. I told Billy I would send him the money, but never did. I have not seen Billy since and he has not seen my $500, either.

What is it like to get cut? I'll tell you. It's terrible. It's a terrible feeling. At that point in my career, I was trying so hard for a job. I was released before training camp was over. The new coach wanted to keep an extra linebacker rather than an extra defensive lineman, and I was the extra defensive lineman. It was hard, because I'd been on the team the year before and had friends on the team, like Pat Fischer. I had to worry about what to do next.

When the Cardinals cut me, I remember talking with Ed Henke again. I played behind him on the depth chart. When Ed found out I'd been cut, he came and talked with me.

"They cut you?" he asked. "Damn it, you're the best player we got. Don't worry. You'll play somewhere."

This really made me a feel a lot better, and then he went on to express the universal attitude of every professional football player with regard to other guys getting cut.

"I feel really bad about this," he said. "But better you than me."

Fortunately, Pop Ivy called me. Pop had been hired to coach the Houston Oilers the next season. He said that he was going to draft me into the AFL, to come play with him at Houston. Pop called and said, "I need you! I need you bad!" My rights in the AFL were owned by the Denver Broncos, so he made a trade to Denver to get my rights, and I went to Houston. I really didn't miss a step. I just moved right into their program.

I showed up in Houston near the end of their training camp. The Oilers trained at Ellington Air Force Base in Webster, Texas. Houston's camp was a little different. The AFL was just getting started, and its teams were picking up players left and right who had just been cut in the NFL camps, players like me. The AFL teams would watch the NFL cut lists and then there would be a mad race to pick up the good players as soon as each was cut before the other teams could get to them. I made it through camp and made the team.

AFL paychecks were small. Everything was done on a shoestring. Paula, Tammy, and I lived in a Houston motel. Our quarterback and kicker, George Blanda, also lived there, with his wife.

I played in four or five games for the Oilers, who were on their way to an excellent 11-3 season and the AFL Championship Game under Pop Ivy. After the fourth or fifth game, a game in San Diego, I went into a migraine seizure. The seizure was scary. When the team got back to Houston, they put me into the hospital and ran a lot of tests on me to try to figure out what the problem was. They hooked me up to equipment that could read my brain waves. In all, the Oilers had me take three electroencephalograms, a test where wires were connected to my head and brain.

After these inconclusive tests were run, I was back in action, but the Oilers didn't really play me after that. I think they were afraid I was going to get really hurt, or maybe even die on the field. And the AFL, being in only its third season as a league, really didn't have the kind of financial resources that the NFL did.

Pop Ivy was very supportive of me. "I'll get you out of here and back on the field," he told me when he visited me in the hospital or while I was recuperating. "You seem fine to me. We need you." But I never got to play. "I don't have any control over whether or not you play," he told me. "I'm just the coach." However, he did keep coming and asking how he could help, and eventually I asked him whether he could get my paychecks for me. When Pop came back, he had my check.

I was released. I packed our stuff, loaded the family into the car, and we drove back to Nebraska so I could do my student teaching. The whole 1962 season had been an exercise in futility. I'd started out playing a full year in the NFL with the Cardinals, but had been released by two teams in less than a year. At this point, I was ready to hang it up. It seemed like no team was interested in me. I heard later that Houston had been telling everybody I had something wrong with my head. I think teams were worried that I would drop dead or need expensive medical care, and there just wasn't as much money for things like that back in the old days.

I knew teams in both leagues were tracking the problems I'd been having. There were letters going around about me. But teams that should have picked me up didn't.

I finally got a call from the Minnesota Vikings. The general manager called me up and told me that they had been tracking my progress medically, were getting various letters from around the league, were willing to take a chance on me, and wanted to sign me. I signed a contract and arrived three days early for Vikings training camp.

Vikings coach Norm Van Brocklin was a different trip altogether. He was an ex–football player, a former Philadelphia Eagles quarterback. He was tough. A lot of former players have not been successful coaches, but Van Brocklin is one of the successful ones. He was a screamer. Guys who played *with* him couldn't stand him, and guys who played *for* him couldn't stand him. I didn't like him and I didn't meet many guys who *did* like him. The guys who *really* didn't like him were the players who had been playing with him whom he then signed to play for him—he treated them like dogs. He was a very hard guy to play for. I could handle the fact that it was supposed to be kind of like the military, but he was insulting as well. If I told you some of the things that he said in this book, you wouldn't believe it. But I won't do it. He made the team run two miles after an exhibition game in Portland. He would also lie to you in a minute.

The 1963 season began with me at my third training camp in two years. I came ready to play, but Van Brocklin would not play me. He wouldn't play me on special teams, or as a defensive lineman, or anything during camp. All I participated in were a few scrimmages. It was apparent that Minnesota had picked up some information on me after I signed, and they seemed hesitant to play me. I got the feeling it was just a matter of time before I'd get cut for the third time in two years.

The first preseason games rolled around, and we flew out to the West Coast for games against San Diego and Los Angeles. They didn't play me as a lineman in either game. I think all I did was play on special teams. When we got back, the Vikings announced the first cut, cleaning out about twelve or thirteen guys, including me. All but one other guy and myself were rookies. Part of the reason I was cut, I'm sure, was that I was playing behind Jim Marshall in the depth chart, and Jim Marshall was one of the greatest defensive ends to ever play the game. But that cut hurt, because I was in the first cut, was one of the only non-rookies, and had played an entire successful season in St. Louis. It was very disheartening. I'd given it another shot by coming to Minnesota, and I'd had the same result.

"I've had about enough of this," I thought to myself. "I've got a family. I just need to go back home and teach industrial arts, and be a schoolteacher."

When Van Brocklin released us, he didn't even bother to show up and tell us in person. He had his general manager come and tell us that we'd been let go and then told our little group, "We have a bus that will be here in a minute to take you guys to Minneapolis." Once we got to Minneapolis, the team would put us up in a hotel for two days and then would pay for us to get home.

I was already not too happy, and I knew that league rules said they had to fly us out of camp. The camp was quite far from Minneapolis, up at Lake Bemidji, at Bemidji State. I got the other guys together after the general manager left. "The rules say the team has to fly us to Minneapolis," I told them. "They do?" asked one of the rookies. "But we don't want to piss him off," said another kid.

"Here's what the rules say," I explained. "Let me take care of this." I went to the GM and said, "I need my plane ticket." "You're going back by bus," he said. "Nope. The rules say you have to fly us out of here if there is an airport available. We fly out of here for all our exhibition games. There's an airport."

He hemmed and hawed for a while, and he finally gave me the Minnesota Vikings' team credit card and told me to go ahead and charge it to the Vikings' account. I went back to the field, where the other guys were waiting.

"We're flying out of here and the flight leaves in one hour," I told my little group, and we went out to the airport. I lined those eleven rookies up behind me at the ticket counter like they were all my little kids and I was taking them all to the movies.

"We need twelve seats," I told the ticket agent. Then I paid the bill and told them that the Vikings would be down later to pick up the credit card. We all piled on and flew down to Minneapolis.

When we arrived, we had to check in at the Vikings' office. There was paperwork to sign. I told the other guys to let me go first and take care of things. They had no idea that the Vikings had given me permission to fly only myself and I didn't want them to have a chance to mess things up. They all thought the Vikings had flown them all down. After I'd taken care of everything, we were supposed to hang around for two days, but I went straight back to the airport and took the next available flight to Toledo.

No one ever called me about that incident. I ran into that Vikings GM a few years later, when he was on the Saints, which is where Van Brocklin went after he got fired by Minneapolis. The GM laughed about it at that point. But Minneapolis was a new team back then, and they didn't have a lot of money. They'd been trying to save a few bucks by making us take the bus. All the teams did that kind of shit. They wouldn't pay for anything if they could get away with it. But I got the best of them on that deal. I've always laughed about that.

I got home and was ready to start my career as a schoolteacher. But things were just about to turn around for me in a big way.

4

The American Football League Changes Everything

People now don't realize how small the NFL used to be. There were only twelve teams. There were plenty of other cities that wanted teams, but the NFL was a hard league to get into. Ralph Wilson was one man who saw how popular football was becoming. Wilson was from Detroit, and his father had made a lot of money selling life insurance. Wilson's father was also the part-owner of the NFL Detroit Lions. Wilson noticed that before people began getting their own television sets, there had been very little interest in professional football outside the areas that had teams. Football was more of a regional sport. There were no teams at all in large parts of the United States. People who lived outside those select NFL cities were much more interested in college football. However, in the late fifties, the prices on televisions started to go down, so more people could afford one, and lots of people began buying black-and-white sets.

When professional football games first started to be televised, people tuned in. As early as 1958, fifty million homes watched the NFL title game between the Giants and the Colts.

Ralph Wilson wanted a team. So did a lot of other wealthy investors around the United States. Down in Dallas, another rich kid, Lamar Hunt, had been trying unsuccessfully to buy an existing team. Finally, Hunt decided to start his own league, which he named the American Football League. In pro baseball, there was a National League and an American League, so why not a National and American League in pro football? Wilson first tried to get the city of Miami, Florida, interested in a team, but they turned him down, so he went to Lamar Hunt, who suggested some cities that might work, including Atlanta, Georgia; Buffalo, New York; Cincinnati, Ohio; and Louisville, Kentucky.

The National Football League scoffed at its new rival. Cleveland owner Paul Brown had no faith in the AFL's success. He said flat-out, "This league is not going to last. It's a bunch of sons of rich guys. It's a hobby with them. They don't know anything about football. The people playing there are not capable of playing in the National Football League. They'll be nothing but cast-offs and they won't last more than a year or two." And he wasn't alone. A lot of people didn't expect the American Football League to last long, and that probably included some of the owners, many of the players, and many of the fans.

The city of Buffalo had hosted a successful pro franchise in the All-America Football Conference, also known by its acronym, the AAFC, but that league had folded in 1950. Ralph Wilson knew that Buffalo was a lot like Detroit—a blue-collar factory city. Buffalo already had a stadium, War Memorial Stadium. The stadium was an old Works Progress Administration Project, built during the Great Depression. It could hold thirty-five thousand people. After Buffalo's AAFC team went belly-up, the old stadium fell into disuse. I think they used it for stock car races. When Ralph toured it, he wasn't too impressed with the facility, especially the locker rooms. It was run-down and needed a lot of work.

On October 17, 1959, Ralph finally got his team. He was now the owner of one of the original eight teams in the brand-new American Football League. These original owners were called "The Foolish Club," basically a bunch of rich guys who liked football and wanted to own a pro team. The original teams were in Buffalo, Houston, Dallas, Denver, New York, Los Angeles, Boston, and Minneapolis. Ralph once compared starting the AFL to starting a new car company from scratch and having to go head-to-head with Ford and General Motors.

The first AFL draft, held in November 1959, was also pretty bare-bones and low-key. The owners simply put all the names into hats based on player position and then they took turns drawing the names out. The first draft went thirty-three rounds.

Wilson also signed a two-year lease for War Memorial Stadium for $5,000 a year and 50 percent of the net proceeds from concession sales. He then recruited a top-flight general manager, Dick Gallagher, and put him in charge of building the team. Gallagher knew how to pick players. As the director of player personnel on the Cleveland Browns, he'd found Jim Brown and Bobby Mitchell.

In January, the Minnesota franchise bolted to the NFL, leaving the AFL with only seven teams. Luckily, Oakland wanted a franchise and quickly got approved. Oakland was then given the former Minnesota team's draft picks. The American Football League had two divisions: the East would include the Buffalo Bills, the Boston Patriots, the Houston Oilers, and the New York Titans. The West would include the Dallas Texans, the Denver Broncos, the Los Angeles Chargers, and the Oakland Raiders. The league commissioner was Joe Foss, who'd been a hero in World War II. The old World War II ace now piloted himself as he crisscrossed the country, promoting the new league.

As Ralph's general manager, Dick Gallagher knew it would be tough competing with the NFL for players, so he switched his focus to getting good players out of the college draft. The AFL made a good league move by deciding to hold their draft before the NFL held theirs, but there was no guarantee this would work. For example, I got drafted by the Denver Broncos, but I didn't sign because I wanted to see what the NFL would offer. Gallagher knew that the AFL would get first shot at the college talent, and he also knew that once the NFL teams held their training camps, the NFL teams would be cutting players, and this would give him an opportunity to pick up veterans as well.

The Bills organization decided to let the Buffalo fans help name the new team. Some of the suggestions, according to Bills historian Jeff Miller, were the Buffalo Nickels, the Buffalo Bison, and the Buffalo Eries. On November 30, 1959, Ralph's team officially became the Buffalo Bills, which had also been the name of Buffalo's old AAFC franchise.

The Bills opened their first-ever training camp at the Roycroft Inn and Knox Estates, in East Aurora, New York, that summer under Head Coach Buster Ramsey. Some names instantly recognizable to most Bills fans played for the Bills from the very first year, including Wray Carlton, Elbert "Duby" Dubenion, and Tommy O'Connell. The Bills' uniforms and helmets looked an awful lot like the Detroit Lions', where Ralph was still a minority owner. The Bills helmet was silver and the home jersey was a pale blue with white pants. The helmet had no logo, just the player's uniform number in light blue on the sides.

While I was still playing college ball, the new Buffalo Bills played their first game September 11, 1960—a 27-3 loss to the New York Titans. Even in its first season, Buffalo made its name on defense, allowing the third-fewest yards in the AFL. The Bills' offense sputtered the first year, and went through several quarterbacks while ending the year with the worst passing offense in the AFL. The running game was a little better, thanks to Wray Carlton and Duby Dubenion.

The Bills ended their inaugural season in third place in the AFL's Eastern Division with a 5-8-1 record. As a business, the Bills were a money-loser in 1960, leaving Ralph Wilson $200,000 in the red. Ralph didn't care. He was pleased with the first season and happy with the fans' support of their new team.

The AFL made a brilliant move in negotiating a joint television deal with the smallest of the three U.S. television networks, ABC.

At $8.5 million over five years, the deal wasn't as big as the NFL's, but it did guarantee income for each club, about $170,000 the first year, with the agreement that it would go up in years to follow. ABC really didn't have a sports wing, so it contracted its sports division to a company called Sports Programs, Incorporated. The main producer was a gentleman named Roone Arledge, who would go on to become one of the greatest television sports producers in history. Arledge had a new vision for the way football games should be telecast. He believed that it was the producer's job to bring the game into the viewer's living room. ABC also started using more than one camera so that they could cut from one camera as the passer threw the ball, to another camera downfield, instead of panning with the ball. Arledge did a lot of things like that, and it made the AFL games more exciting to watch. And unlike the NFL, the AFL did not insist that cameras cut away from the game if there was an injury or a fight.

The AFL had wide-open offenses. Sid Gillman, who coached the Chargers, used a brand-new offensive scheme, where instead of using the run to set up the occasional pass, he used the pass game to set up the run. And Sid influenced a lot of future coaches, like Bill Walsh, Chuck Noll, and Al Davis. Passing games were more fun to watch and more exciting. Down in Houston, my old teammate George Blanda was enjoying the AFL passing game. He'd played ten years in the NFL for the Bears. When he signed on with Houston, he'd been working for a trucking company. The guy ended up playing until he was forty-eight years old—twenty-six seasons—and it was the AFL that had given him new life. The AFL was much more fun for a quarterback. The NFL played a ball-control game while the AFL believed in the pass. The AFL did a lot of things first, and that changed the game of football, making it more exciting and fan-friendly. For example, they were the first to put a player's name on the back of his jersey, and the first to link the scoreboard clock to the official game time. They also used the two-point conversion from the college game, and were much better about recruiting black players. They were the first to have their games nationally televised, the first to use portable TV cameras and on-the-field microphones, and as well as the first to have their games broadcast in color.

5

The Bills, Year One

To really understand the Buffalo Bills in those years in the mid-sixties, you have to know about our coach, Lou Saban. Lou was a former collegiate and pro player who dedicated most of his life to the craft of coaching football. He coached collegiately before becoming coach of the AFL Boston Patriots. Saban's peak as a coach came during his first tenure in Buffalo, which began in 1962. During this period, Saban led the Bills to two consecutive AFL Championships. This was followed by stints at Denver and a return to Buffalo, as well as many years of coaching college teams, Arena League teams, and even high school teams. He coached twenty-one different teams in his career, but would never again experience the success of the Buffalo Bills' early years.

I'd only been home in Toledo about three days when Lou Saban called me. The first call came from Harvey Johnson, who was the Bills' personnel director. Harvey was an ex-coach, and he and I became good friends. When I got his call, I had already accepted a job teaching school in Toledo, but it wasn't time for school to start yet.

"I'm calling for Lou Saban and the Buffalo Bills," Harvey said, in his country accent. "We're really excited to see you. I just saw you on the wire. What's the situation?" I said, "They just cut a bunch of us in Minnesota, and I just got back into town."

"All we need is one more defensive end," Harvey said. "We

played against you down in Houston and we think you're really good. If we can get one more good defensive end, we can win the championship."

"Well," I said, "I really appreciate you thinking I'm that great, but I've never heard of one player being the difference in winning a championship, especially a defensive end. If I was a quarterback, maybe that would be a little different."

Harvey kept talking to me. "I don't really know if I'm interested," I finally told him. "I'm a little shell-shocked about football at this point. "Okay," he said. "Well, Lou Saban will be calling you," and he hung up.

And sure enough, Lou called right back. Now Lou's a different kind of person. He's optimistic. He told me, "Oh, come on! We need you bad! You got just what we need in Buffalo!" Lou repeated what Harvey had told me: if the Bills could get a good defensive end they could win the AFL Championship. Lou could sell you anything. He was persistent.

He wanted to fly me to Buffalo, but I couldn't make the connection, so I went by train from Toledo, and then drove up to the training camp at the Camelot Motor Inn in Blasdell. It was empty. Some of the players had gone to play an exhibition game in North Carolina. I found out my first roommate (for a day) was to be Jack Kemp, the Bills' quarterback. He was also gone on the road trip. When the team got back, Coach Saban introduced me around to some of my teammates, and I tried to find out why the Bills had taken a chance on me when no other team seemed willing to do so. As far as I could find out, the Houston Oilers' general manager, John Breen, and the team, had blackballed me due to my migraines. He sent out a letter to all the other teams telling them not to pick me up.

Lou asked me how much I'd been making in Houston, so we could get the contract taken care of. I'd made $9,250 as a Cardinal, and then $10,000 at Houston. I told Lou $15,000. Lou said, "No way!" I said, "How about $10,500?" Lou then said he'd do

$11,500. What was I going to do? I needed a job. I signed the contract and it was sent to the league office.

The league rejected the contract. I did not know for a long time the details of the contract rejection. There was a newsman in Buffalo by the name of Jack Horrigan. Apparently, Horrigan called Saban and said, "McDole has a bad head and we cannot sign him." Lou called me in and said, "We can't okay this. The league is worried about a big lawsuit if you die."

The AFL was still almost brand-new, and it was broke. It simply could not afford a lawsuit. I think this is what kept me from playing for Breen in Houston. In my opinion, Breen wanted to make sure that if I didn't play for the Oilers, that I also would never play for any of the Oilers' opponents.

I was examined by the Bills team physician, Dr. Joseph Godfrey. They hooked up my brain with wires and ran all kinds of tests, just as they had in Houston, and I passed all of them. Lou told me he'd never trusted Breen. He's just trying to keep a good player out of the league. Lou called the Bills' owner, Ralph Wilson, in Detroit.

"He's a good football player," Lou told Ralph. "We could really use him. He's passed all the tests." Wilson said, "Sign him!" I was officially a Bill.

The Bills' training camp was an interesting place. The team headquarters was also at the Camelot Motor Inn, which was located on Mile Strip Road overlooking the New York State Thruway near exit 56. The motel made us two practice fields out back, and surrounded them with snow fences. They also gave us a little space out behind the building to build a locker room and equipment room. Our trainer, Eddie Abramoski, and some of the Bills staff built it. We used the motel ballroom for meetings. Sometimes, we'd go up to the ballroom and walk through our plays. Fans could come watch free of charge. The Camelot had TV in the rooms, and air conditioning, as well as a food service. It had only two stories, so a lot of players snuck out. Sadly, the old motel and facility were torn down in the eighties and were replaced by a shopping center.

Funny story. One year my roommate, George Flint, picked me up to go to camp. He was from Pennsylvania, so he drove from Arizona, where he was living, and came and picked me up in Toledo, and off we went. However, he told me that we had to stop by near Erie, Pennsylvania, to see his uncle Amos and his grandmother. "Everyone gets upset if I don't stop and visit," he said, "since I'm a big star in my hometown."

We pulled into Erie, and George headed for his first stop, Uncle Amos. He'd have a place for us to sleep. And we also had to go see George's ninety-year-old grandmother, who was slightly senile and lived outside of town.

I noticed as we pulled up to Grandma's house that she had a big old shiny Packard sitting in the driveway. Going into her house was like going back in time, filled with dainty antiques that she possibly bought new. She asked me to sit down, but I didn't see a chair whose lumber looked up to the challenge of supporting me, so I stood.

Before we knew what hit us, Grandma had us going to the supermarket with her to pick up a few things. We insisted that we had to get going, but she wouldn't hear of it.

When we'd climbed into Grandma's car, George had a worried look on his face. She was behind the wheel, and George let me know that she wasn't allowed to drive any more.

We walked out to Grandma's Packard, and I got in the back seat. I am no dummy. She gets in the driver's side, starts it up, and floors it. We go screeching out of there, right through the red light. We come to the main drag, and Grandmother whips out into the road, takes a left turn, never slowing down, traveling down the highway, makes two more turns, flying, goes roaring into the grocery store parking lot, slams on the brakes, and comes to a screeching stop right in front of the store. She then calmly gets out.

She throws the store door open and we walk inside. I see three or four people start moving around quickly, and then she starts down the aisle. Grandma eats an apple off of the shelf, and she discards items behind her that are picked up by an employee right behind her. Grandma then buys a couple of bags of stuff, we go out to the car, and we're off again at warp-speed. I don't remember anything about lunch in Erie, Pennsylvania, but I'll never forget George's shoplifting, hot-rodding grandma.

I was very fortunate, at this juncture in my career, to play for a coach of the caliber and temperament of Lou Saban. I've played for four or five different coaches, and the two that stand out to me are Lou Saban and the Redskins' George Allen. They were both totally dedicated to the game of football. They put a lot of time into the job. They were students of the game. They embarrassed you because they spent so much time. They'd spend hours breaking down plays on film. George was all about football, twenty-four hours a day, year-round, and Lou was kind of the same way. They were both great leaders. They had a knack of moving players and coaches around, knowing their players, handling their players. One person you can holler at, and he'll play better; another you holler at, and he quits. A good coach is a psychologist. Lou was a big factor in our success. He was strict, but he treated his players like adults.

He understood not only the game but how to get the best out of his players. Lou and George both knew how to handle *people*. They were family type of people. They were smart football people, though George was probably smarter. He'd study stuff to death. Lou was all about "we are a big family," and he was a team guy. The players were more important to him than the owners. It was the same with George. They could get the right players together, and then get those players to really *play* for them. Once you get everyone believing in you on a team, you can't do more than that. The biggest problem teams have, in my opinion, is they get split up and you get cliques. And suddenly you got everybody out for themselves, each group for itself.

Lou knew where to put people, too. For example, he moved Tom Day. Tom was a big guy who had played defensive end in college at North Carolina A&T. When he came to the AFL, they moved him to offensive right guard. Lou moved Tom back to right defensive end. Since I was new, Lou put me at left defensive end. We both ended up playing the rest of our careers at the positions Lou had figured we were the best at.

Lou also had a great situation in Buffalo. The owner, Ralph Wilson, was a nice guy. He stayed out of the coach's way and let him make the decisions.

One time, we lost our defensive line coach, and Lou jumped in to coach the defensive line. We had a lot of fun with that. Lou would walk over in his blue sweat jacket and start doing these offensive line drills with us. In one of the drills Lou would set himself, and we were supposed to run up and shake his shoulders and try to get around him. We used to just shake the *hell* out of him! We'd throw him on the ground, and he'd get so mad! We'd say, "Well, you want us to do it right, don't you?" After a while, Lou started to spend less and less time coaching us.

I was working that first Bills season for $11,500. Contracts in the old AFL or NFL were pretty ironclad. You were basically owned by a team for life unless they released you or traded you. This was before the era of big money attracted agents. I had only one agent my entire career, and his name was me. The only players who had agents back in the early sixties were guys whose fathers were already lawyers. The rest of us negotiated our own contracts. And contracts back in those days could get creative.

For example, one year in Buffalo, I "negotiated" a $500 raise by building horse stalls for the Bills' personnel director, Harvey Johnson, who was a big horse track man. I told him I'd do it, but I'd need a tub filled with ice and beer, and that I figured it would take me a day or two. By the end of the first day, I was all done, and I left. Harvey called me up and said, "Wow, what a beautiful job! Fantastic! How much do I owe you?"

"Five hundred," I told him. He said, "Five hundred?! That's outrageous!" I said, "Okay, then. How about giving me a $500 a year raise and we'll call it even?" Fine, he did. He gave me the raise. That way he paid for his stables with team money rather than his own.

During my first off-season with the Bills, I spent some time as a substitute teacher, making seventy-five dollars a day. At the time, I was in Toledo remodeling my parents' duplex. My old shop teacher called me up and said, "We need an industrial arts and PE teacher in the low-income section of town, at two junior high schools." In one school, I taught shop Monday and Tuesday, then Wednesday I taught grades one through eight in physical education. I taught shop at the other school on Thursday and Friday. These schools were in an old, tough neighborhood. One of the schools was in the middle of a block, a great big school, with a small play-yard outside, and the school was surrounded by old homes. When we played baseball, we were always hitting the ball into these two old ladies' yards. I'd have to go beg to get the ball back, and finally they just refused to give the balls back. I went to the principal and told him about this. He told me to make a new rule that any ball hit over the fence was an out. Well, that wasn't any fun. But the ladies would not give the balls back. Finally, I went to the principal and told him that I needed more balls.

"Why?" he asked. I told him, "All my balls have been stolen." He asked, "Stolen? By whom?" I said, "By these two little old ladies across the street."

The principal looked at me and said, "So, you're a big football player and you're scared of some little old ladies? This is your problem, not mine." I ended up trading yardwork to get the balls back.

We also had the Presidential Physical Fitness tests. I had to run these in the spring, go out there with my stopwatches and clipboard, and write down everybody's scores on all these different physical fitness tests. Well, some of the kids in the school were three grades behind. They just kept flunking over and over. And they sure as hell didn't care about any physical fitness test. So, I sent a bunch of kids out on the six-hundred-yard run, told them what time they had to beat, and so forth, and off they went. Some of the guys I sent out on the run didn't come back, about six of them. I waited a long time and they didn't reappear, so I had to go search for them. I found them in a sweet shop halfway around the block drinking pop.

In Ohio, kids were put in different classes based on intelligence. I had one class that was very low. And one of the physical fitness tests was the potato race (also called the shuttle run). A runner runs from one line to another, picks up a potato, returns to the start, puts it down, runs back to the second line, gets another potato, and runs back over the finish line. It took me *three days* to try to teach this one class how to do the potato race. And when we'd run it, I'd say "Go!" and the kids would run off and forget what to do. We finally gave up on the potato race.

I was the only man in the school, other than the maintenance man. I had a nice shop. We built racks for all the tools, and painted the silhouette of the tool on the pegboard behind the tool. That way, we could always tell if a tool was missing or wasn't put away. Well, somebody was stealing tools. One day, I stood up in front of the class and said, "We're missing some tools." Nobody fessed up. But the next day I caught a kid stealing a tool. I had a nice paddle, wooden, with holes in it, and I paddled that kid right up there in front of the class. Then I said, "I hope this cuts down on the tools disappearing."

I went to the principal and told her what I'd done. She said she'd deal with any fallout from the parents. A few days later, I get called on the intercom. "Mr. McDole, Mrs. Johnson is here with her son." I was worried. How would it look for this big football player to be beating the shit out of a kid? When I got to the office there was this big black lady looking at me like she was going to kill me.

"Sorry I had to punish your son, Mrs. Johnson," I said. "I caught him stealing tools." Mrs. Johnson said, "You can whip his ass any time you want. His father took off and since then I can't do anything with him!" What a relief.

Now I had a new problem. All the other teachers wanted paddles. I made it a shop project. All the shop kids had to make these nice wooden paddles for the other teachers, had to label them and everything. The kids weren't too thrilled about having to make those paddles.

I also had an interesting experience with the intercom in my room. A week after I started teaching, I heard a "click." I had no idea what it was. Then, a week or two later, the principal said something she would only have known if she had been in my classroom. I found out where the intercom in my room was, and I climbed up and disconnected it. A week later, a maintenance man from the school district showed up and said, "I have a work order here to fix your intercom." So, he climbs up and checks it out. He said, "Well, what do you know, the wire's come loose. Hmm." And he fixed it. As soon as he left, I disconnected the intercom again.

A few days later, the maintenance man is back. "Do you leave your room unattended?" he asked me. "Why?" I asked. He said, "Because the wire has been disconnected again. Do you have kids climbing around in your room when you're not looking?" I told him, "No. I don't think so."

A week or so later, he was back again. "Well, now the wire is *completely missing*," he told me. "I'm tired of coming back over here every week and fixing this damn intercom."

I looked at him and said, "Why don't you just tell the principal that the intercom can't *be* fixed?"

It took him a minute to figure out what I was saying, then he nodded. He told the principal he had to call in and special-order a part, and of course the part never came in and the problem was solved.

Another great experience I had that year was when I taught a group called Sight Savers. The school took the kids who couldn't see very well and paired them up with sighted kids. The sighted kids would run the machinery and help the other kids do their projects. And the best projects were from the kids who could not see, because they had this tremendous sense of touch, and their work was always smooth and carefully finished. The sighted kids would try to pass off the blind kids' work as their own, but that didn't fly.

Having two leagues did mean there were a lot of players in the mix and a lot more jobs available, but it also meant that the two leagues had to compete for the best players. Was this a good thing for players or a bad thing? I think it was a little of each. I remember asking my University of Nebraska friend Mick Tingelhoff, who'd been drafted a year after me by the Vikings, what the NFL players thought about the AFL. "Well, let me put it to you this way," Mick told me. "There are a lot of guys here in the NFL who are glad to get a job. And there are a lot of guys in the AFL that can take them."

The competition for talented players between the AFL and the NFL meant that, for the first time, there was a bit more of a free-market feel to being a professional football player. Then, when the AFL got its first national television contract, the league also became much more appealing to some big-time players, some of whom signed with the AFL right out of college. The first four or five AFL years, agents just weren't that popular. About the time the leagues merged, the era of money was just beginning. That's when the agents showed up. Agents want 10 percent of something worth getting. Who wants 10 percent of $11,500? There were some bad agents, greedy ones. They would steal money from guys or get them locked up in bad contracts. Eventually, I think most agents got 10 or 15 percent of the player's salary, and later, 10 or 15 percent of a player's earnings on and off the field. If you did appearances, if you did commercials, they got a percentage of that as well. Some of the agents got way out of whack and so the league stepped in through the NFLPA and said that agents had to be licensed. I recently received a flyer from the NFL Players Association, and it was just shocking to see how much money the players are making. The top players were getting from $68 million to well over $100 million. And some of that was guaranteed. We were never guaranteed money when I played.

In the very first game of the season, one of the players got hurt, and I got to play. That was the beginning.

The year 1963, my first year in Buffalo, was also a big year from a historical standpoint. That summer, we watched the March on Washington, where Dr. Martin Luther King Jr. gave his famous "I Have a Dream" speech. As football players, we were still very aware of the evils of segregation when we went south to play games.

The Bills played in old War Memorial Stadium, fondly known as "The Rockpile." It was an old stadium, with none of the amenities one associates with modern professional sports. One week, the Bills were going to be playing a game on national television. Naturally, the team wanted its venue to look good to the viewers around the nation (and ABC wanted good-looking football fields). War Memorial Stadium was also a baseball stadium, and it had a pitcher's mound and a dirt infield. I don't mean just the base paths were dirt—the *entire infield* was dirt! We often used that infield to our advantage in football games. Jack Kemp would throw passes to his receivers near the dirt spot where the pitcher's mound normally was so that the defenders would trip and fall. Since we had that ugly infield, the stadium folks knew we had to get it taken care of before we were on national television.

First, they tried to seed it. They had some new kind of fast-growing grass, and they seeded the entire infield. The next day when we showed up to practice, there were hundreds of pigeons out there eating the seed off the field. The team decided to put guys from the city workforce in the stands with pellet rifles to scare off the pigeons while we used the field for practice. We had ten maintenance people sitting up in the stands shooting in our vicinity the whole time we were trying to focus on practice. Finally, we yelled at the crew, "Get 'em outta here! They're going to kill us!"

The grounds crew tried mixing poison into the grass seed to

discourage the pigeons. When we showed up for practice the next day, every one of those pigeons was laying there dead on the field. Hundreds of dead pigeons! Our trainer, Eddie Abramoski, raised pigeons as a hobby, and he ran out onto the field checking the bands on the pigeons' legs, to see whether any of them were his. Instead of practicing that day, we spent the time going around with big garbage bags bagging up all the dead pigeons.

Their next idea was to spray-paint the infield green, and that's what they did for the television game. Not only was the field green, but our uniforms were green by the end of the game.

All our facilities were different back in those days. Nowadays, you go to any NFL facility and it's like being in the world's best sports club. The new pro facilities have everything from swimming pools to state-of-the-art weight equipment. There are two or three trainers, and a doctor who comes in regularly. Not so in those days.

In the winter time, it gets frigid up in Buffalo. When we practiced in the winter months, we had these large tubes that the field tarps were rolled up into. These took up a lot of space, so we'd practice in a smaller area off the main field. On cold days, guys would go hide in the tarp rolls to keep warm. Heck, sometimes we'd be missing half the team because it was so cold and they'd all crawled into the tarp rolls trying to stay warm.

In Buffalo, we did not have a regular practice field. One time, they had us go get dressed in our uniforms, and they had buses waiting for us. We got dressed and climbed onto the buses and then drove around Buffalo trying to find a decent park to practice in. When we found one, we'd park the buses, pile off the buses, and go practice.

We practiced in the armory in Buffalo near the stadium several times. We had to go over there and run between the tanks. We'd be practicing, and our quarterback, Jack Kemp, would say, "Go down by the Jeep, cut left, and I will hit you at the tank!"

Near the end of my tenure in Buffalo, around 1970, we even practiced at a hockey rink, on the ice. Everyone was slipping around falling with tennis shoes on. But that was just what we had to do. Buffalo was one of the worst in the league for facilities; they did not have any money, and we had nowhere to go.

I watched, listened, and learned, both from others and from experience. As a backup, and as a former offensive lineman, I played against all these great defensive ends, and I tried to learn how to be an effective blocker. This, in turn, made me a better defender. There was an old guy named Perry, and he taught me a great trick. "Reach inside, grab the jersey, and pull the player down to the left or right and fall. The officials won't see it." And he was right. There were a lot of tricks like that I learned from guys or learned myself. For example, there was very little passing in the college game when I was there, just running with the occasional pass to keep you off balance. So most offensive linemen didn't have to pass block very much. On a pass, most offensive linemen would sit back a little bit in their stance and you could see that. If they sat back, just a little, you could pick up on that and know a pass play was coming.

The more you studied guys in their stance, the more you looked at them, it got to the point where I could read a lot of times whether a guy was going to pass block or run block.

I also learned that offensive and defensive players have different personalities. Most of the time, I can walk into a room and look at a guy and can tell whether he's an offensive or a defensive player. I can pick out a defensive player with ease. Defensive players tend to be outgoing, rowdy. Offensive players tend to be more quiet, reserved. I always considered Len Hauss, the Redskins' center, as a defensive player at heart.

There were a lot of characters on the Bills. It was a close bunch. We were a bunch of guys, most single, but a few of us married and with kids, and we didn't make a lot of money. We all worked in the off-season, had no choice really. We really were like a family. We hung out together, and our wives hung out together, and eventually our kids hung out together.

The Bills had been aggressively signing players for the past year, and they were feeling like it was just a matter of time before they became successful. Their first few years for the team were not bad, but not great, either. In 1960 they were 5-8-1. In 1961 they improved to 6-8. In 1962 they posted their first winning season, with a record of 7-6-1. They'd picked up quarterback Jack Kemp from San Diego, and signed fullback Cookie Gilchrist and receiver Ernie Warlick out of the Canadian Football League. Both Gilchrist and Warlick were already stars in Canada. The Bills also had some good rookies, like Tom Sestak, who had been drafted out of McNeese State. The team had a very good wide receiver in Elbert Dubenion, who'd played for them since the beginning and would become one of the all-time greats. Saban also brought some real talent onto his coaching staff. He changed our ugly uniforms, which Wilson had originally made to look like the Detroit Lions', into something with some flair. Lou's new design was blue uniform jerseys with red and white piping and white pants with piping. The helmet was white and had a red stripe down the center. On each side was a new design, a red silhouette of a buffalo.

We lost the first two games of the season, then tied Kansas City, then lost again to the Houston Oilers. After the third game, which was our home opener, our fans were throwing beer cans at us! The fans in Buffalo let you know what they thought. They were hardworking people and they expected the same out of their football team. They loved the players, but they'd be honest with you, too. In Buffalo, if we had a bad game, you would hear about it. There was no escape. George Flint saw a little old lady hit one of our guys with a cane on the ramp leading onto the field. But the fans were also extremely loyal and good to us.

To get an idea of how much the fans loved the old AFL Bills, I wanted to include the recollections of a lifelong Bills fan by the name of Mike Faley, now a record producer in California, but at the time just a football-crazy kid with a dad who encouraged that love. The Bills were part of Mike's growing-up, and they remain a big part of him today.

Said Faley, "The sixties were the golden age of football, filled with legends like Y. A. Tittle, Bart Starr, Johnny Unitas, Jim Brown, Gale Sayers, and many others. But *my* heroes were Jack Kemp, Cookie Gilchrist, Ron McDole, Tom Sestak, Tom Day, Jim Dunaway, 'Golden Wheels' Elbert Dubenion, Glenn Bass, Wray Carlton, Daryle Lamonica (the Mad Bomber), and others. You were in Bills country, and Bills fans took their football seriously. One year our kicker Booth Lustig missed a 19-yard field goal against Houston in the final seconds and was MUGGED later that night! We are talking about hardworking, hard-drinking, blue-collar fans supporting a hardworking, blue-collar team, armed with our hot dogs and buttered popcorn, and extolled to 'get your ice-cold Genesee beer here!'

"Buffalo's front line was a BEAST. Forget the NFL! I would put that 1964–65 defense against any NFL team and that team would be in a world of hurt! McDole, Day, Dunaway, and Sestak was a front line you could not run on, and held every team to less than 66 yards a game those years. You could hear the hits in the stands. Fans yelled for DDDDDD-fense and they wanted blood! The owners had to put chicken wire over the exit in the early days to get the referees out alive!

"The Buffalo defense of 1964–65 is, in my opinion, even better than our Super Bowl defense with Hall of Fame member Bruce Smith. It was not a defense of superstars—they were a team, our team. God, I miss that team."

George Flint agreed to pick up my paycheck for me one week. He had to pick it up at the Bills' office in downtown Buffalo. On his way out, the wind got my check and blew it away. I wasn't too worried. Either it would get lost or somebody would turn it in. Sure enough, an elderly lady brought my check in to the Bills' office. I went in to pick it up.

"Did you get her name?" I asked. "I'd like to call and thank her." And when I called her, her first comment was, "Is that all the money you make?!" Well, it was a weekly rather than a monthly paycheck, but it still wasn't very big.

One incident that stands out from 1963 involves a promising young rookie running back, Roger Kochman, from Penn State, who'd been activated because of nagging injuries to Gilchrist and Carlton. Kochman had some very good games, after rushing for 99 yards against Houston on September 28, and then 60 against Oakland the next week. On October 13, he had 86 yards rushing, 3 catches for 80 yards, and a touchdown against the Chiefs. On October 20, we played Houston again, and in the second quarter, Kochman hurt his knee very badly. It was absolutely the worst injury I saw in my eighteen-year career. They found out later that basically everything in his right knee was severed except the skin. Our team doctor hadn't flown down with us, but he put us in touch with the best surgeon in Houston, who at that time was Dr. Michael DeBakey, who would later make many improvements to the heart-bypass procedure.

As a rookie, the kid didn't have a lot of resources. The surgeons had to rebuild his entire Achilles tendon, as well as operate to prevent having to amputate his leg. Bills owner Ralph Wilson stepped in. Ralph had quite a bit of money, thanks to his insurance business, and Ralph picked up the whole tab for Kochman's medical treatment. The injury was career-ending, so Ralph paid Kochman's tuition to go back to school. That's just the type of guy that Ralph was. Normally, he was hard to get money away from. I know from my own experience he was tough to get $500 from. But in the case of Kochman, Ralph showed what a generous and good man he truly was.

We still had the original eight teams in the AFL, but two teams saw some changes. The New York Titans changed ownership and became the New York Jets, but still were one year away from moving from the Polo Grounds to Shea Stadium in Queens. And the defending AFL champions, the Dallas Texans, moved to Kansas City and became the Kansas City Chiefs. We didn't win until October 5, against Oakland. Starting with the Oakland win, we went 7-3 the rest of the season to finish at 7-6-1. The first year on the Bills was important to me. The year 1963 was the first time I got the opportunity to play. All the Bills players, in fact all the AFL players, were kind of in the same boat. It was a new league, new people, and everything was changing so fast. When they picked me up, I was at the point where I thought that I'd probably never get to play professional football because of my migraine situation.

The year 1963 was tough for the nation. In November, we lost our young president, John F. Kennedy, to an assassin's bullet, and in our national grief, professional football history and American history crossed paths again, in ways that would change the game. The president was killed on a Friday, November 22, and the NFL decided to go ahead and play its games two days later, on Sunday, November 24. NFL commissioner Pete Rozelle was friends with Kennedy's press secretary, Pierre Salinger. Rozelle spoke with Salinger, and Salinger told him that he felt that the NFL should go ahead and play. By doing so, the NFL could show that the country continued to function as usual and boost public morale.

In contrast, Bills owner Ralph Wilson was adamant that the AFL should cancel its games that week, and discussed the matter with AFL commissioner Joe Foss. Wilson later told newspaper reporter Scott Pitoniak, "It was a slam-dunk that we shouldn't play [and] fortunately, Joe Foss agreed with me. Some of my fellow owners were on the fence at first, hemming and hawing, but I was resolute. . . . If the commissioner had forced us to play, I probably would have taken a forfeit—and we were in the playoff hunt at the time."

Later, NFL commissioner Rozelle called his decision to go ahead and play games that weekend the biggest mistake of his thirty-nine-year tenure as league commissioner.

6

Back-to-Back Championship Seasons

The Buffalo Bills became a success in 1964 and 1965, winning back-to-back AFL Championships. In 1964, we went 12-2-0. I started all fourteen games and I got the first interception of my career, as well as not one but 2 safeties. In all, I scored 10 points—6 on an interception touchdown, and 4 on the safeties. Not bad for a big defensive lineman. In 1965, we went 10-3-1. Again, I started all fourteen games, and had an interception, which I returned for 24 yards, and 5 fumble recoveries.

But the individual statistics mean nothing to me compared to the Buffalo Bills' back-to-back AFL Championships. How did we do it? We played as a team. We took turns making the big plays. If one guy was down, another stepped up. And we had some very, very good players.

Still, there are not many Buffalo Bills from that era in the Hall of Fame. Why do you suppose that is? I'll tell you. It's because Buffalo was a team on which everyone just did a good job. There were no superstars; instead, everybody took turns.

During the early and mid-sixties, we had a defense that was one of the best in the game. This included a solid front four: Tom Day, Jim Dunaway, Tom Sestak, and me. Sestak was an amazing athlete out of tiny McNeese State (the AFL made it a point to find talent at smaller schools). Tom was the big cog of our defensive line—a great ball player who could get the job done, no doubt about that. He had his knees beaten up pretty bad over the years but he still played. He did not even practice the last two years of his career, just played in the games. Practice beat up his knees, and he had to save them for the games.

In the off-season, Tom and I liked to go up to Canada with Doc May, who was a veterinarian friend of mine. We would go up to some cabins in the off-season and go fishing. He loved to fish. Tom is gone now, but his son Tommy remembers those annual fishing trips up to Canada. "When the boys needed a break, they went fishing in Canada, and took me. After a private flight in on a dual-prop pontoon plane we'd land in Thunder Bay. We had a cabin on the beach. I remember thinking how big Ron McDole was. Both he and my dad were huge and I was only eight at the time. The first night there was so fun. My parents and the McDoles sat around laughing, talking, eating fresh food, drinking beer, and playing dominoes. Ten good days. Giant lake trout and muskie. Ron and Dad were best buddies."

Tom, he gave it everything he had, and boy, he did not like sitting around. If he couldn't play, it was highly unusual. When he did play, you knew he was hurting. This was a shame because Tommy was still a young man, but his knees really got bad and finally forced him to retire. We were the guys up front and we were not little people.

Tom was a quiet guy but a hell of a football player and a great friend. His tolerance for pain was amazing. Man, he was tough! He never bitched about anything, he never complained, and he never raised his voice.

Our defense went 17 games when no team scored a rushing touchdown on us. We also had a very good defensive secondary with Mike Stratton, Harry Jacobs, and John Tracey at linebacker, Booker Edgerson and Butch Byrd at cornerback, and Hagood Clarke and George Saimes at safety. In 1965 Hagood had 7 interceptions, and Edgerson and Byrd had 5 each.

We had a good offense, too. Jack Kemp may not have been the best quarterback in the AFL, but he was a great leader on a team that played as a team and didn't depend on superstars.

Cookie Gilchrist was another great player. He was our full-back and the AFL's first 1,000-yard rusher in 1962, and was also named that year's MVP. Cookie led the AFL in scoring every year he was on the team. But he was hard to control at times. He was always getting into a scrape.

The Bills' offensive line was a good one, anchored by the great Hall of Famer, Billy Shaw and right guard Al Bemiller.

I played with a lot of receivers and tight ends in eighteen years, and two of the best were Elbert Dubenion and Glenn Bass. Glenn Bass was an excellent player—just a quiet player who did his job. Same with Duby. He was consistent and dependable, as was our tight end, Ernie Warlick. Everybody did his job. Nobody stuck out. It was the ideal football team. And that's why we were so successful.

We had several new defensive ends in training camp who had been high draft picks, but Lou told me that the job was mine until I lost it. And going into training camp, I knew I had to do my best. One of the new rookies at training camp was a kid named Hatch Rosdahl. I believe he'd been the Bills' number-two draft pick. He was about 6 feet 6 inches and looked just like a Greek god, with chiseled abs and huge muscles.

Jim Dunaway and I are both rather fleshy, and neither one of us looks like a Greek god. Neither of us liked to lift weights, and we rarely did. This stayed the same my whole career.

So, Jim and I were sitting in the weight room talking one day. Rosdahl came up and lifted some huge amount of weight, and he was cocky. He said, "I'll bet you guys can't lift that much weight."

Jim and I looked at each other. Jim said, "Sure I could, if I felt like it, but I don't." Rosdahl said, "I'll bet you can't do it." Jim shrugged.

Later, we were outside standing near a chin-up bar, and Rosdahl came up and began doing pull-ups, one after another. Finally, he dropped down and smirked, "I suppose you can do that, too, can't you?"

Jim looked at Rosdahl and then at the bar. "Well, I could, but

I prefer to do my pull-ups with one hand." Rosdahl laughed. "Sure, you do."

So, Jim jumped up, grabbed the bar with one hand, and did twenty-one one-handed pull-ups. Then he jumped down and looked at Rosdahl. I was a little worried that I'd be expected to do pull-ups too, but Jim's performance was the end of Rosdahl's cockiness.

Our punter was Paul Maguire, who also played linebacker. Maguire was a jokester, always playing pranks. Now, it was the first day of a big training camp scrimmage, and all the rookies got there early. This was their first chance to show what they had in a game situation, and they were eager to make a good impression. About ten minutes before the scrimmage starts, here come these two fat guys, McDole and Dunaway. You could hear us coming up the stairs, boom, boom, boom. We walked in and all these rookies looked at us like, "This is the great Ron McDole, this big fat guy? And this other big fat guy is the great Jim Dunaway?" They were shocked.

Then Maguire, who was already there, piped up, "You should have heard these guys talking behind your back before you two got here! They said you guys are big and fat and they're gonna knock you both flat on your asses in the scrimmage!" The rookies looked up at us wide-eyed. "No, we never said that!" "We swear!" "Maguire's lying. He's trying to get us in trouble with you."

And Dunaway was standing there, not saying a word, looking at these rookies out of the sides of his eyes, really scary-looking, as if he'd like to kill them. Never said a word the whole time. And I said, "Aw, Jim, I think Maguire is just making this up." But Jim kept staring and those kids were scared to death.

Dun was born in 1941 in Columbia, Mississippi, and played his college football at the University of Mississippi, where he was a unanimous All-American. The 6 feet 5 inches, 280-pound giant was the third player taken in the 1963 NFL draft, picked by the NFL Minnesota Vikings. Instead, Big Jim opted to play for the AFL Buffalo Bills. Dunaway was a four-time All-Pro in the AFL, and was part of the vaunted Buffalo defensive line of Day, Sestak, and me, and was my longtime roommate. He was traded to the Miami Dolphins in 1972 and played on the legendary undefeated 1972 Miami Dolphins team that won Super Bowl VII against the Redskins. He was a four-time AFL All-Star and a two-time AFL champion (in 1964 and 1965), he played on the Miami 1972 Super Bowl team, and he ended his career in the World Football League with the Jacksonville Sharks and the Jacksonville Express before the WFL folded.

Jim retells it: "In Buffalo, we had a good defensive line in the mid-sixties. I think we still hold the record for not letting an opposing team score a rushing touchdown in seventeen games.

"One thing I remember about Ron is that he could eat! One thing you could not do around Ron was, do not order pizza! He would get a head start on you by starting to eat it when it was still really hot—so hot it would burn your mouth. He ate it anyway. On the plane, he'd get a little steak and before I even had mine, he'd given his plate back.

"Those days back in the AFL in Buffalo were different from the way things are done today. Our training camp at the Camelot in Blasdell, just outside Buffalo, was a good example. The food was horrible. They fed us wiener soup so many times we finally said, 'Hell, no, we're not gonna eat it anymore!' and we boycotted the Camelot restaurant. They finally started serving food you could recognize. Getting in shape meant mostly running. The camp was in a pasture behind the motel. The only weights I saw were some free weights, and the only guy I saw using them was Tom Sestak, who would lift the weights and do some exercise with them behind his neck. We had one chin-up bar, and one bag we could hit. Coach Saban was the defensive line coach. Occasionally we used a seven-man sled.

"The main way we got in shape for the season was by incrementally playing more. We'd play one quarter in the first preseason game, two in the second, three in the third, and by the fourth we'd play the whole game. We got fifty dollars a game for playing preseason games. The pay was not very high in those days. The low- and high-end pay for a man on the offensive or defensive line would be $10,000 a year and $15,000 a year.

"All players back in the day had a second job. You had to. And football wasn't a year-round commitment like it is today, so you could do that. In 1963, I started farming in Mississippi. I farmed cattle, hay, and all that. And I bought more land as I could and at one time owned 1,700 acres. I bought a dairy and did that for twenty-seven years. I had 300 milk cows that all had to be milked twice a day and 150 head of half-Brahma beef cows. Add in the 40–50 replacement heifers and dry cows. It was a big operation and a lot of work."

Trainer Eddie Abramoski is one of the few of the guys who were there at the very beginning. The man is a living legend, and his name is on the Buffalo Bills Hall of Fame. Ed worked as head trainer from the team's inception in 1960 until his retirement in 1997—a span of thirty-seven years. Eddie remembers Jim and me and our adventures with food well.

"Ronnie and his Bills roommate, Jim Dunaway, were notorious eaters. There was a restaurant in Dunkirk, New York, called Rush's. Rush's offered a special: 'All the lobster dainties you can eat for one price.' We were training nearby, at Fredonia, New York, and the team had a day off. Ronnie and Jim went to Rush's and ordered the all-you-can-eat lobster dainties. They ate sixty-two lobster dainties between them. The manager was miffed. After they'd finished, he asked them whether they were going to have dessert. 'What do you have for dessert?' they asked. 'Strawberry shortcake,' the owner said. 'We'll take two each,' they told the owner.

"But come game day, Ronnie led by example. He showed little emotion. His attitude was just 'do it!' He was a big guy, but he was so fast, and he'd run all the way across the field and tackle a quarterback for no gain. It would be third and one, and the runner would go the opposite way, and you'd see Ronnie running across the field, full speed, and he'd tackle the runner for a loss."

The Buffalo Bills were cheap, and Maguire wanted some new footballs to punt. Punters and kickers are very picky about having newer balls to kick, but the coach told Paul he still had plenty of balls and that the ones he had still had plenty of use left in them. Maguire didn't want these older balls. We were practicing at a park, and there were hundreds of kids watching us from behind a chain-link fence. Maguire took those old balls one at a time and punted them to the kids, one after the other, twenty-one balls in all, until they were all gone. Then he got new balls.

The 1964 season was an unbelievable year. We had a couple of other guys who were cast-offs who came to the Bills that year. Some were veterans, but a lot were young guys just trying to prove who they were. That whole run of time, from 1964 into 1966, we performed with all cylinders firing, and it was possibly the best, most exciting time I ever had.

The 1964 and 1965 Buffalo Bills were total underdogs both seasons, but we had great people and every week we got the job done. The entire 1964 season, whenever we needed a big play, someone stepped up, and we did it with a small roster of thirty-three players. Thirty-three guys who either did not get signed or were released from other, mostly NFL, teams. And despite the perceived lack of respect for the American Football League, with its crummy stadiums and low payrolls, we all truly felt both years that we could play against Green Bay or any NFL team. We had unity and we had a great coaching staff. We played at a consistently high level. The team finished with a record of 12-2, the best record in the AFL. We nailed down the division in the snow at Fenway Park, beating the Boston Patriots, 24–14. Thousands of fans cheered us at the airport upon our return.

Jack Kemp was a natural leader on and off the field. To him it was all about the team. He kept Cookie Gilchrist in line, which was a job in itself. Jack and I remained good friends, even when he got to elected to go to Congress in Washington. He was there when I played on the Redskins.

Jack and I used to carpool because we lived close to each other up in Buffalo. I would drive one week and he would drive the next. I always had to stay late on Wednesdays, because the offense would have extra meetings after practice and Jack was always the last to leave.

One Wednesday after practice, a friend of one of the players drives up to the training facility in a semi-truck filled with color televisions. Color TVs are fifty dollars! Wow! Color TVs for fifty dollars gets everybody scrambling to get fifty bucks.

Jack walks in to the locker room and Jim Dunaway, who has run into the locker room to get fifty dollars out of his locker for a TV, tells him about the great deal. "You're not going to buy one of those TVs, are you?" Jack asks Jim. "Hell yes!" says Jim. "You do know they're stolen, right?" Jack says. I walk up to them. "How do we know they are stolen?"

As Jim and I buy our TVs, Jack keeps saying, "You are committing a crime." I say, "I am not committing any crime, Jack. I am just buying a TV." Jack begins lecturing me left and right. Then he says, "You're not going to leave, right?" I say, "No. I'm waiting till you're done, but I want to go down and get a TV and put it my car. I'm not going to leave you."

Jack keeps repeating over and over, "You are committing a crime. You're are just as bad as they are." I say, "I don't care. I'm going to get down there and get my TV before they're all gone!"

I start off down the steps. Jack hesitates, then says, "Here's fifty dollars. Get me one." I say, "What? That's just as bad as what I'm doing!" Jack says, "Well, I don't want you to go to jail by yourself."

We never did get our TVs. They arrested the guy before we could get one.

We faced the San Diego Chargers in the AFL Championship Game. The Chargers were the defending champions, everybody expected them to beat us. Bookmakers made them 14-point favorites. Nobody really believed in the Bills that year, except maybe our fans. After all, Buffalo was a young team, a team made up of a revolving door of former NFL players, deemed not good enough for the NFL—too old, too short, from a smaller college, too slow, you name it. The running joke on the team was, "Don't send your clothes out to be cleaned." We had no delusions of greatness. We just wanted to play football and were thrilled to be there. We had no real stars, but we all worked like hell. If the coach said he needed us to play the other way, we would have stayed up all night learning the playbook. Every player had heart.

The Chargers had a lot of offensive stars, players like Lance Alworth, Tobin Rote, and Keith Lincoln. They had a tough defense —the front four were nicknamed the "Fearsome Foursome"— before the LA Rams took the name a few years later—and they were huge. Ernie Ladd was 6 feet 9 inches and 290, and Earl Faison was 6 feet 5 inches and 270. They were a very, very good team. Even before the game started, they were talking trash. Faison came into our pregame huddle and told us he was going to kill us.

The biggest play of the 1964 game came during San Diego's second drive of the game. The Chargers were already up 7–0 and were driving. Quarterback Tobin Rote dumped a screen off to Keith Lincoln. Mike Stratton anticipated the play and hit Lincoln just as the ball arrived. Lincoln was down, and out. He had to go out of the game with broken ribs. That turned the momentum in our favor. Coach Saban said later, "The Stratton hit actually turned the key. From that point on we felt we did have a chance to win it. Mike's hit was a display of defensive strength. It lit the flame." We won the game, 20–7. We were the American Football League champions!

Mike Stratton is one of those great Bills all the old fans remember. Stratton was drafted in 1962 in the thirteenth round out of the University of Tennessee by the Buffalo Bills, and played linebacker in the American Football League and National Football League for twelve seasons, first for the Bills, then for the

San Diego Chargers. He was a six-time AFL All-Pro. In an interview we did in 2015, Mike shared the following: "Every time the ball came to my side, I knew I could expect Ron McDole was coming from the opposite side. He would not quit. He did not quit. He was immune to pain while he was playing. When you can play as long as he did under the circumstances he played in, with the extreme body makeover he'd had to make in college, it was amazing. He was durable. Optimistic. And he enjoyed fun.

"If you were playing football for the money, you were going to be disappointed. But we were there to do the best we could when it was our time to do it.

"We used to park our cars in the lot of Loblaw's grocery store near the stadium. That whole area in Buffalo was a very old neighborhood, and not the best. Most people who could afford to were moving to the suburbs in the sixties and seventies.

"After 1966, the Bills didn't really have a good team. Some years, we could hardly wait until the last game of the season. Ron was there during the fun years, but missed some of the tough ones near the end.

"Ron's strength as a player, if I had to pick just one thing, would be . . . no, I can't do that. He had many strengths. He was one of those guys who had the ability to see things in his mind. I don't even know if he knew it, but he could always do it. He could focus. Ron was like this. All-out. That got him all the admiration from the rest of the defense and the whole team in general.

"I played linebacker. Ron made many of the tackles on my side of the field, the right side, and he was a left defensive end.

"I'm proud to know Ron. If anyone deserves to be in the Hall of Fame, Ron does. As great and durable as he was. His name is the first name that comes to mind when I think about who deserves to be in the Hall of Fame. Doug Atkins is in the Hall. Both Doug and Ron played the same years and Doug has been in the Hall for a long time.

"There is a certain amount of NFL snobbery. Billy Shaw is the only AFL player who had his entire career in the AFL to be in the Hall. And that's sad. The old AFL players are going to be in our eighties soon, and then, it will be too late."

Speaking of Billy Shaw, he may be the greatest player the AFL Bills ever produced. He's the only player who played his entire career in the American Football League and is in the Pro Football Hall of Fame in Canton, Ohio. A graduate of Georgia Tech, he was drafted by Buffalo in the fourteenth round as the 184th pick in 1961. During his playing career—all with Buffalo—he was named to the AFL All-Pro team eight years in a row, from 1962 until 1969. In addition to being in the Hall of Fame, he is on the AFL All-Time Team and the Bills Wall of Fame, and he was named to the Bills 50th Anniversary Team.

Billy remembered the Bills years with me in a talk we had in 2014, which I'm sharing here:

"I was a number-two draft choice, and signed with the Buffalo Bills prior to the NFL draft. In the NFL draft, the Dallas Cowboys drafted me in the fourteenth round, as the 184th pick. The reason I signed with the Bills is that the Cowboys wanted to play me at linebacker and I'd never played linebacker. The Bills said that they would play me as an offensive guard.

"The American Football League was only one year old. The Cowboys, and a lot of others, believed that the AFL would fold. People don't realize that in the early years of pro football, our roster was only thirty-three guys. That meant you practiced against your first-team defense every day. The Bills had the best defense in football for a number of years, from 1964 to 1966. I have to give the Bills defense all the credit for the growth of our offensive line and our entire offensive team. We literally practiced against the best.

"My last season was in 1969, which also happened to be the AFL's last year. I'm the only Hall of Famer who never played a single down in the NFL. There have been thirty-five, or maybe a little more, players who are in the Hall of Fame who played in both the AFL and the NFL, but I'm the only AFL-only player. There are some guys who played in the AFL who have the credentials to be honored in the Hall of Fame. Ron is certainly one of them. By the way, there is no such thing as the NFL Hall of Fame. It's called the *Pro Football* Hall of Fame.

"I first met Ron after the 1960 college season at the Senior Bowl. We were both seniors—he at Nebraska and I at Georgia Tech. I saw his ability in that game and made a mental note, 'Hey, this guy is pretty good!' When he joined us, all the memories of that game came back to me, and I thought, 'I remember this guy!'

"He's exceptionally quick for such a big man. He has great movement, quickness off the ball. He has the ability to move laterally. He could have played professional football as an offensive guard and been a really, really good guard in addition to being a great left end. He was dominant because of his quickness.

"His ability to move was his greatest asset. He had an ability to elude a tackle with movement. I watched him do it all the time. I was on the sideline watching while he played. When the game started, he wasn't the fun-loving, joking guy he was the rest of the time. He was a serious, serious, football player. Every play was for real. He had 12 career interceptions, a pro record for a lineman, not just because of his quickness but because he knew where to be on every play. That's not easy to do. You always need to know the correct pursuit route for each play. He was a student of the game. He knew his opponent. He had a different game plan for each tackle he played against.

"From 1962 until 1966, I was the offensive captain and Tom Sestak was the defensive captain. In 1967 I got hurt and missed five or six games. I think in 1967 Ron and Kemp were captains.

"Ron was a natural team captain. He was a consistent player. But the captain also had a very important job on the Bills. We served as a liaison between the players and the coaches. If there was a disgruntled player, you carried his side to the coaching staff. The reason men were picked to be captains was not just their ability, but the fact that they had the trust and respect of the players and the trust and respect of the coaching staff. Ron had all these characteristics. And he was a leader on the field.

"My fondest memories of Ron are his contributions to our success as a team. He was such a dominant player. I have great respect for him."

Thanks, Billy. The feeling is mutual.

Though not remembered nearly as well as Stratton or his bone-crushing hit on Lincoln, another Bills player by the name of George Flint was another big reason we were AFL champs and is also a prime example of a player stepping in and stepping up to help win a crucial game. In the 1965 championship game, George had to line up against the great Ernie Ladd, and Flint played Ladd straight up.

Flint had an interesting story. He was from Pennsylvania, but went to college for a few years in Arizona. One day, George and a few of his friends got drunk and they all went and joined the Marine Corps. He was in the Marines for a few years, and when he got out, he started playing football again. George told everyone that he was only twenty-one, but he was a good deal older than that. He was an old-school utility player who could play any position; he would do whatever it took to stay on the team. He knew that most bench players wouldn't last two years if they didn't start. And George made a career out of being a utility backup player. He'd do whatever anybody needed him to do whenever anybody needed him to do it. One swelteringly hot day, we were scrimmaging. George had been in for ten minutes and finally got a break. He ran off the field, sweat pouring off of him, hot as hell, and said to me, "Man, I need a break!" The next second, the whistle blew, his name was called, and he ran right back in. He did whatever it took to keep that job.

George was never a star, never got big money, and occasionally it showed. George liked to dress kind of country. He had this old rawhide jacket. He and I roomed together on road trips for several years. One time we flew out to Oakland to play a game, piggybacked with a game the next week at San Diego. We were waiting in Oakland for our bags at the baggage carousel, which was a new thing in those days, and we saw this ratty old straw box bound up with rope going around and around on the carousel. All the players and other passengers loitered at the carousel after getting their own bags. They were all curious to see who this hillbilly suitcase belonged to. George and I stood there waiting, too. Finally, we had to go get on the bus, and still nobody had claimed this ratty old straw box.

After we got settled in at the hotel, George said, "Let's go rent a car!" "Why?" I asked him. "We're gonna be here all week, we might as well have a car," George insisted.

I didn't want to, but we went and rented a car. After we got in, George looked at me and said, "We're going back to the airport. That was my bag." He hadn't wanted to claim it in front of everybody else. He was too embarrassed. I doubt that would happen in the NFL nowadays.

Years later, when I played on the Redskins, Flint got me good. Duke Ziebert, a Washington restaurant owner, used to bring cake and ice cream out to Redskins Park to get publicity for his place. One day, I was sitting in the sauna eating ice cream, my big belly hanging out, and somebody took a photo. George was there visiting and he saw the photo and stole it. Later, I went to see George's dad in Arizona. There were seven or eight guys sitting around in a bar, and George had blown that up photo of me eating ice cream in the sauna and mounted it on the wall over the bar.

In 1965, the AFL crossed paths once again with the tumultuous history of the nation. The 1965 AFL East-West All-Star Game was scheduled for January 16, 1965, at Tulane Stadium in New Orleans, Louisiana. A month before the game, the Supreme Court ruled that the Civil Rights Act of 1964 forbade racial discrimination in motels and hotels. But when the black players showed up for the game, they found it difficult to get a cab, eat in a restaurant, or stay in a hotel.

At the airport, most of the cabbies wouldn't pick the black players up. Some players waited up to three hours to get a cab into town. Eddie Abramoski, the Bills' longtime trainer, remembers that some cabbies did pick up black players, took them twenty miles out into the country, and dropped them off. Three Bills players wanted to visit the French Quarter. Two were white, one—Ernie Warlick—was black. The cabbie wouldn't let Ernie in the "whites-only" cab.

After Ernie Ladd and some others were threatened in a Bourbon Street nightclub by a man with a gun, Ladd had had enough. Ladd, one of the most dominant defensive players in the game, along with the twenty-one other black players, including the Bills' Ernie Warlick and Cookie Gilchrist, voted 13-8 to walk out of the All-Star Game that year in protest.

In a sign of solidarity, the white players backed their teammates up, including Bills Jack Kemp and Billy Shaw, as well as Coach Lou Saban. The AFL moved the game to Houston. It was an example of athletes—black and white—standing together against racism.

The year 1965 was also the year of Joe Namath. "Broadway Joe" signed what was then the biggest contract for a rookie in pro football history. Back in the sixties, there were maybe thirty players a team, making $10,000 to $20,000 apiece. Joe was the $400,000 man. That's probably well below the current NFL minimum. Plus, current teams have seventy to eighty players, and every one of them makes a big paycheck. The name of the game is money. Owners spend as much as they can to put the best team on the field. That in turn gets them fat TV contracts, which makes the owners more money, and so on.

A salary of $400,000 sounded like a lot back then in the AFL, but the Jets also had an owner with a background in Hollywood who was used to paying actors hundreds of thousands of dollars. He got Namath out of the University of Alabama and paid him a lot of money and that's where the escalation of wages really began—that and the end of the unwritten rule between leagues that they would keep their hands off of each other's players.

Joe Namath was a great athlete. He and George Blanda had the quickest releases. It was frustrating as a lineman to rush a quarterback who could get rid of the ball that fast. Joe sometimes gets a bad rap. He didn't sign autographs while he was eating or doing something where he wanted privacy, and some people disliked him for that. But he would sign forever if he wasn't busy, especially for kids. One time, at the All-Star Game in Jacksonville, Joe sat out on the field and signed autographs for at least an hour for every kid that wanted one.

Another pivotal event in the rise in player salaries was when our placekicker, Pete Gogolak, signed with the New York Giants. Gogolak was a soccer-style kicker, the first to play in the pros. When the Giants signed Gogolak, they violated an unwritten rule that the NFL teams and the AFL teams would not sign each other's players. Also, ABC had been broadcasting the AFL games. It wasn't until NBC picked up AFL for the 1965 season that the money got better.

We started the 1965 season as the American Football League champions. Offensively, we lost Cookie Gilchrist in a trade to the Denver Broncos, and Wray Carlton took over the rushing duties. We picked up Paul Costa, a rookie out of Notre Dame. He'd played running back in college, but Coach Saban turned him into a tight end. He was a big guy, and it was a natural fit. Costa could arm-wrestle, too! He beat everybody on the team, even Jim Dunaway!

We also had two very good quarterbacks—Jack Kemp and Daryle Lamonica. Coach Saban used both that season. We lost Elbert Dubenion early in the season, and Ed Rutkowski became our new go-to receiver. Early in the season, we beat Boston, Denver, New York, and Oakland before our first loss against San Diego. We rebounded and beat Kansas City and Denver, then lost to the Oilers. Then we won against Boston, Oakland, San Diego, Houston, and Kansas City. We lost the last game of the season to the Jets, but we were already in the playoffs.

Our defense that year gave up a league-low 226 points, only 16.1 points per game, and we led the league in interceptions, with 32. We extended our streak of games in which we did not allow opponents a rushing touchdown. This streak began in week six of the 1964 season and extended through the AFL playoffs and championship, then through week eight of the following season—a record that's never been beaten. We finished the 1965 season 10-3-1 and defeated the Chargers 23-0 in the AFL Championship Game.

I had a good year, playing in all fourteen games. I picked up my second interception that season and made 2 safeties, a stat in which I led the league. I got the interception against the New York Jets, the day they played their last game at the New York Polo Grounds, and the day before they tore down the Polo Grounds. My first interception, I was playing behind a Jewish player named Sid Youngelman. Tom Sestak, our star tackle, got kicked in the head and knocked cuckoo. I was put in at Sid's position, and Sid moved over to tackle. On the first or second play I batted the ball down. That first interception set me on my way to one of my professional football records—most interceptions by a defensive lineman. I finished my career with 13, as well as 3 safeties, 16 fumble recoveries, and quite a few blocked kicks. They didn't keep track of sacks in those days, so we'll never know how the old players did in that department.

In 1965, we played Namath and the Jets, and all of us guys on the defensive line created a sack pool. We each threw in ten bucks and the winner would be the guy who sacked Joe for the biggest loss. I won that one after I caught the poor guy fifteen yards behind the line of scrimmage. He kept backing up as if he didn't think I could catch him. After I sacked him, Joe looked up at me and said, "How'd you catch me?" I guess he thought those white shoes made him fast, or that I was too fat. Sorry, Joe. I won the check pool!

I do not think a modern player would have lasted for five minutes, during this time, the way we trained and played. We trained hard, played hard, and had great coaching. We won as a team.

Nobody in the United States believed that we could beat San Diego in the AFL Championship in 1964—and we beat them in 1964 and finished the season ready to repeat!

When we flew out to San Diego for the rematch in 1965, the Chargers still had a roster of stars and were again huge favorites to beat the Bills. We got there a week early and prepared hard for the game. All week we heard how our win the previous season had been an upset and a fluke and how the Chargers were a better team and were going to thrash us. We had three injured wide receivers, so Saban went with a double-tight-end formation with Costa and Ernie Warlick. We also had to move Al Bemiller to center due to an injury to Dave Behrman. We had a strong, adaptable offensive line, and despite the changes, we remained confident.

The gameday weather was great. But shortly after the game started, our star guard Billy Shaw got knocked out of the game. That's when George Flint, Mr. Utility, came in to line up against the human mountain, Ernie Ladd. Ladd had about one hundred pounds on George, but Flint played a hell of a half. It was 14–0 at halftime, and Billy came back in the second half. We ended up shutting them out, 23–0. Two championships, back-to-back. Jack Kemp was named AFL MVP, and we had numerous guys make the All-Pro team. I think that may have been one of our best wins ever.

Unlike today, those days saw players staying on the same team year after year, and that gave teams a cohesiveness lacking on modern teams. Nowadays, it's a money chase. Players change teams so often that it's hard to get any consistency. That Buffalo Bills' team was tight. We hung together, played together, and socialized together. Here we were, playing in a league they never thought would last, many of us NFL rejects, thumbing our noses at the NFL.

We didn't make a lot of money. In those days, if you played professional football, you had a job in the off-season to support yourself. Paul Maguire and Tom Sestak had a restaurant in Cheektowaga called Sestak-Maguire's. Al Bemiller and I had a construction company, Tammany Construction, and we built houses, entire subdivisions. Some of the Bills players ended up living in our subdivisions. We gave them a discount. Eddie Abramoski, our trainer, bought a house we built and lived in it for over forty years. He reminded me that when he moved in, Paula and Wanda Bemiller were dusting and cleaning the windows. The Costas and the Rutkowskis lived there, too.

Since I built houses for a living in the off-season, I used to load the family in the station wagon and we'd go look at old houses for fun. We found an old house in Eden, New York, that I loved. The Schweickart house was an old brewery on one hundred acres, and we bought it from the family for $30,000. The historic old house needed a lot of work. I figured I could spend years fixing it up.

It was still a few years before the Bills got our first big superstar, O.J. Simpson, but the writing was on the wall. Owners were finding that they had to pay more for players, and began rethinking their own game plans. Two leagues meant bidding wars. The NFL owners began to think that maybe a merger with the AFL wasn't such a bad idea.

7

The Famous Buffalo Bills Halloween Parties

The Bills were a tight team, and we had fun together. Lou Saban fostered a family atmosphere. One thing the Bills did that became the stuff of legend was the annual Buffalo Bills Halloween party. Joe Auer, a former Florida Gator, had the first party. After Auer, the Maguires hosted it, then Paula and I ended up throwing the rest of them.

Most players in Buffalo rented their homes, but Ernie Warlick, Al Bemiller, and I bought an old corner house over in Grand Island, between Niagara Falls and Buffalo. We bought it from a church across the street, and it was big, and spooky-looking, and surrounded by large trees. We lived in the house while we remodeled it into apartments. We started having the parties at our place because the players had a habit of kind of tearing things up, causing problems with the landlords.

Our biggest problem with throwing a Halloween party was that often, we couldn't have it on Halloween because we had a football game to play. We worked the party around the games—sometimes we had them before Halloween, sometimes after. When you play pro football, you have to be a bit flexible with your holidays. You may be playing on Thanksgiving, or Halloween.

The rules were simple. No one was invited except players and family, and no press was allowed, so we could get together and have a good time by ourselves and not have to read about it in the paper the next day. The goal was a party for all of us to get together as a team and have a good time by ourselves. Jack Kemp was already considering a career in politics and needed to be discreet. The only time the press ever came was when a reporter came with O.J. Simpson one year.

The Halloween bash was a costume party, and it was mind-boggling how involved everybody became in having just the right costume. Some people worked on their costume the whole year during the off-season so that when Halloween rolled around, they'd win for best costume.

I was the leader of the costumes, and took my role very seriously. I had all kinds of costumes. One year I was a ballerina. Unfortunately, that year the party was two days before Halloween. Maguire picked me up for the party in my ballerina dress and tutu and little fairy wings, and then we had to stop and pick up somebody else, and after that we stopped for gas at a gas station in Hamburg, New York. It was a cold day and the other guys' costumes were covered up by their heavy jackets. I was sitting in the front next to Maguire. We were just sitting there talking about the upcoming game when the station attendant walked up to the car and saw me—this big guy in a tutu, with fairy wings, a long wig, falsies, and lipstick. I looked like one of those guys that dresses up like a woman. The other guys in the car did not look out of the ordinary.

Paul rolled down his window to talk to the station attendant. "Who is this ugly broad?" the guy asked us. If you look at the photos, I think I look quite cute. I tried hard not to let it hurt my feelings.

The rules called for couples, either a player's wife or girlfriend only. As people showed up, part of the mystery would be to try to figure out who each couple was. We gave prizes for the best costume and for any costume that prevented everybody else from recognizing the wearer. That was hardly ever done. One year, Jack and Joann Kemp traded spouses with Eddie and Marilou Rutkowski and nobody could figure them out. It was always a great time and a great release and the tradition went on for years. We had a lot of fun and *everyone* participated! Very rarely did someone not show up.

One year, it was almost time for the Halloween party, and Maguire was going as a turtle. We'd built the shell with roofing shingles, but as usual we'd waited until the last minute. We were making sure it fit Maguire, down in my basement. Strapped on his back, his shingle-shell was massive; it must have weighed fifty or sixty pounds. Our house on Grand Island always had lots of garter snakes around it. In fact, when it got warm, the snakes got active. My son Taz liked to catch the snakes and sell them. Anyway, Maguire had just put on this gigantic turtle shell costume when Taz walked up and asked him, "Have you seen the snakes all over our basement?"

Maguire was deathly afraid of snakes. His eyes got big and he shot up the basement stairs and never touched one of them! He forgot that he had his turtle shell on, and when he shot up the stairs, he ripped the railing right off the wall. At the party, his shell somewhat repaired, Maguire found that his shell was heavy. As the night went on, Maguire got shorter and shorter from the weight of his costume. He finally took it off. But we have a hilarious photo of him sitting with his little green flippers sticking out, resting, his head poking out of his shell.

Later, when we moved to the new house in Eden, it was the perfect venue for a big party. It had a widow's watch on top, and it was out in the farm country near Eden, New York. On the hundred acres, we had the house and two barns, and when people showed up, it would already be dark. It was scary just driving up the long drive. One year, John Tracey and his wife Beth showed up dressed in corn stalk costumes. They had to come early to put on their costumes, and they went and hid behind the barn and waited for the other guests to show up.

Players took turns choosing the band and the type of music. That year we hired a black band. The band showed up in two cars, commenting on how haunted and scary the house looked, and I told them to park over by the barn. They came running back, "God damn, there are corn stalks running around out in that field!" The girl singer went and locked herself in the car and wouldn't come out for a while. A good time was had by all. The band ended up staying three days. In fact, one or two of them might still be there.

One of the all-time best costumes was one of Joe O'Donnell's. Joe came as Big Bird one year. It was uncanny. He looked as if he had just walked off the set of *Sesame Street*! Joe and his wife Caroline worked on it all year. Another year, some of the black guys on the team came as KKK members, with their white sheets. They burned a cross on our front yard and neighbors called the police to report a cross-burning.

I may be biased, but I always naturally thought that my costume was best. One year I was the Great Pumpkin. I got my costume all built, and it was neat, one of my best. But it was so big I could not get down the stairs to the party. So people had to come up in groups to see me in my costume.

One year I wanted to go to the Halloween party as the Big Chicken. We'd heard a Big Chicken commercial on the radio and that's what I decided to be that year. As Paula recalled, "we were working on his chicken costume in our back yard. Highway 75 runs about 100 yards from our back patio. Ron was standing out there in big yellow tights, and we'd gotten a bunch of feathers from nearby chicken farmers, and we were gluing the feathers on. He also had a glove to put on top of his head like a comb, and big yellow fins for his feet. He had a beak, too. When we went outside to fluff up the feathers and make them stick we noticed cars were stopped and lined up on the highway as far as you could see."

I had to look like the biggest-ass chicken in the world. And at the party, every time I walked up to somebody, they put their hand over their drink so that my feathers wouldn't fall in!

8

The Slow Decline, 1966–1968

We entered the 1966 season as two-time defending AFL champions. This year, the stakes were higher. If we could repeat as champions this season, we would get to represent the AFL against the NFL champs for the so-called World Championship, eventually known as the Super Bowl. We played several exhibition games that year against NFL teams, but during the regular season, we still played as two separate leagues. For years, people had been debating which league was better. Now, we could find out.

Early in the 1966 season Lou Saban resigned as head coach and was replaced by our defensive coach, Joe Collier. The AFL had a new commissioner that year. Joe Foss was replaced by the Oakland Raiders' coach and general manager, Al Davis. Davis did not want a merger with the NFL. When we found out that our kicker, Pete Gogolak, had been signed by the Giants, violating the unwritten poaching rule between the two leagues, the AFL retaliated by signing NFL players. Al Davis contacted all the AFL owners and told them to look at their rosters. Anybody on the roster that the NFL might sign should be signed by the AFL to a two-year contract immediately, which meant you owed the team two years, with an option for a third year. If you moved to another team in your third year, you had to take a 10 percent pay cut. I think Pat Fischer used his option when he left the Cardinals to play for the Redskins, and took the 10 percent cut. This was before free agency. I ended up signing a two-year contract for the same money I'd been making. The two-year contract was for $30,000.

Also, when the leagues began the process of merging, contract calls began in the off-season. Before, a team didn't call until the last moment. It was a bidding war.

The two leagues held secret meetings to arrange an AFL/NFL merger in early 1966. They agreed that starting in 1966, the NFL and AFL champions would play each other in a "World Championship" title game—the words "Super Bowl" hadn't been invented yet. They also agreed to hold a common draft in 1967, and there would be preseason exhibition games between AFL and NFL teams beginning in 1967. One June 8, the merger went through. The leagues would unite for the 1970 season with the NFL's Pete Rozelle as commissioner. Another change for 1966 was the movement of the goal posts from the goal line to the back of the end zone. CBS and NBC got the rights to televise the first four AFL/NFL Championship Games for $9.5 million. The price of a thirty-second commercial during Super Bowl I was $42,000, which, adjusted for inflation, is around $280,000. A thirty-second commercial today costs $3.5 million.

Most of the guys knew every other guy in the AFL and NFL back then. It was a tight little community. You knew everybody either from playing with or against them in college, or through mutual friends. Even the big stars like Joe Namath were this way. Ray Abruzzese, who'd played on the Bills with us, had also played with Joe at Alabama when the Tide won the 1961 college title under Bear Bryant. In fact, Ray and Joe had been roommates. Ray was traded to the Jets, so when the Bills were in town Ray and Joe would meet up with us. Joe paid more for parking than we paid for an apartment. We went out to Toots Shor's with Joe and this was when he was like God in New York. He double- or triple-parked his car, and we got out and he said, "Let's go!" and we just left the car there. We went in and had dinner and drinks and came out and the car was still there, double-parked, door open, ready to go.

One game, we were playing the Jets at home. Our front line was huge. We had Sestak and Dunaway and me, all around 300 pounds, and we had Tom Day, who was about 250. We all hit Joe at about the same time. Joe usually dropped backed up in the pocket and Dun and I came from one side and Ses was on the other and we hit him and knocked him flat on his back. He probably had about 1,000 pounds on him. We never tried to hurt the quarterback, and after we got up and Joe got up, he looked at us and said, "Jesus Christ, did you pass *anybody* up there in a green and white uniform!?"

Namath used colors to call audibles—blue, green, yellow, and so on. We did not know which one was live, but I noticed he liked yellow a lot. You always looked for little things like that when you are playing somebody. Some guys would look where they are going to throw the ball, some guys would do this or that, same thing with running backs. When he passed that color, he could not check off to another play, because everybody would shift on that color.

We were playing in this game and we figured it out, and when he checked off, I moved back into pass coverage. I was so excited because I had never done this in a game, and I got out of my stance and started backing up, and I started stumbling. The more I kept stumbling the faster I was moving trying not to fall on my butt. I was a little bit nervous, excited, because I knew I could get an interception or knock the pass down. I could see his eyes. I didn't fall but I stumbled back in a hurry, and Joe threw the ball right to me. I caught the ball, made about ninety moves, and got one yard. I was only about ten yards off of the line and got killed because everyone jumped all over me. After the game, Joe comes up after his interview and I say, "I appreciate you throwing that pass to me."

"I was not throwing the ball to you," Joe says. "I was throwing it to the tight end, but seeing you running backwards, I knew you were going to fall down. It made me laugh so hard I couldn't get anything on my throw!"

Joe was kind enough to share some of his memories of our times together: "*Roland* McDole, which is what I always called him when I wasn't calling him 'sir' out of respect, was a fine gentleman to me, except when he got a hold of me on the field. He weighed around three hundred pounds. You did not want to be under him when he fell on you. Roland was a gentle giant.

"When I was a freshman at Alabama, they stuck me with a senior roommate from Philly named Ray Abruzzese. Ray ended up playing in Buffalo with the Bills, and I got to know the Bills through him. When the Bills came to town or when we went up to play in Buffalo, we'd get together—Ray, Roland, Tom Sestak, a few others, and I—and we'd go out together.

"I knew Roland from the many times we competed against each other on the field. But I also knew him off of the field because of Ray. We'd all get together in New York City or Buffalo and focus on our 'game plan.' Ron remembers that I used to double- or triple-park in New York City. That's partly his sense of humor, but I think it *did* happen. The owners of the night spots we'd visit had agreements with the people that wrote the tickets. And remember, too, that traffic was light late at night, so it wasn't like it would be today or during the day then.

[When asked about the Bills' sack pool won by Ron in one game, where the defensive line all threw in money and the one who sacked Joe for the biggest loss won the pot] "I don't remember Roland ever getting close enough to touch me except after the game when we shook hands. [Ron won the sack pool, sacking Joe for a 15-yard loss.]

"What made Roland such an amazing player, aside from his size, was his footwork and his quick hands. That, and the fact that he was a great competitor."

Another man who was there at the AFL's beginning and who has enough stories to write his own book is Frank Ramos. Frank was the public relations director for the New York Jets from the team's inception until 2002—a total of thirty-nine years. During this time, Ramos worked for seven owners, seven presidents, five general managers, and eleven head coaches. When I talked to Joe, he recommended I ring Ramos as well, and I'm glad I did. Frank still lives in New York City and continues to be a fountain of knowledge of all things Jets and AFL/NFL.

Frank remembers: "The way players would get together in the old AFL days would never happen today. In those days, whenever the Jets played in Buffalo, the Bills guys—Day, Sestak, McDole, some of the others—would come over to our hotel to visit the Jets players the night before the game. They'd have some drinks and then go out to dinner together. And the next day, they'd go out on the football field and beat each other's brains out! I think it was because it was such a special bond between the AFL guys. They were all united in a common cause, that of the American Football League. There were only eight teams back in the beginning, and everybody from the owners to the players was dedicated to one cause—getting the league established. They all heard how they weren't as good as the NFL, but they all knew guys whom they'd played against in college who played in the NFL, and they knew that they were just as good. It was something to see the guys from two teams gathering at the bar for drinks and then going out to dinner the night before the game! And then go pound each other the next day!

"Ron is as good a player as ever played in the AFL or the NFL. He's one of the AFL players who just doesn't get anywhere near the recognition he deserves.

"There were a lot of stories of old War Memorial Stadium in Buffalo. The stadium had been used by the old All-American Football League team, the Buffalo Bills, for years, and it was an instant stadium for the new AFL Bills, but it was rickety and run-down. The locker rooms were right next to each other and the walls were paper-thin. Weeb was convinced there were spies in that stadium listening in at halftime. He'd talk about a play that the team was going to do in his normal voice, then lower his voice and tell the team the real play. Paul Brown also did this. He'd say a play loud and then repeat the actual play soft. Weeb learned a lot from Paul Brown. He'd been Paul's assistant in Cleveland with the Browns and at the Great Lakes Naval Air Station. Believe it or not, both Paul Brown and Weeb were college quarterbacks, which is surprising in Weeb's case, because he was quite short.

"In the early days, the games did not start until two in the afternoon in New York because of the Blue Laws, which the religious lobby had gotten through so that football games wouldn't interfere with people going to church. Nowadays, there are games at eleven in the morning, but two was late enough that players could go out late the night before the game. The home guys had no curfew the night before the game. They didn't have to show up until ten, when Weeb had a big 'snack,' which was basically a meal. You could even have beer at the function. Then you'd take your beer to a short fifteen-minute meeting and then head over to the stadium later. Players showed up with hangovers, which would not happen today, with all the emphasis on nutrition. Plus, nowadays if you play football, it's a ten-month job. In the sixties, you were done till the next year on the last game of the season. Some players would finish the game, stay in Kansas City, and then fly straight home from the game without ever going back to the team's home city. I'm pretty sure Buffalo did that often, because they ended their seasons in warm-weather cities.

"The AFL had such a strong camaraderie. The owners were close, because they had a common interest. Everybody knew he was an underdog. But he also knew better. He knew he could play against NFL competition. When the Jets won the Super Bowl, we had a big party after the game, and many players from other AFL teams showed up and said 'Thank you! You made us legit!'

"Another example of the camaraderie in the AFL happened one year during the pro draft. The draft was during the season in those days, in November or early December, and the NFL and the AFL drafted on the same day. I was sitting up in Buffalo at the Club 32, where the Bills used to eat, when the sports came on the television. It was announced that the Jets had signed the great Matt Snell, the top pick in the college draft. The Buffalo crowd in that club started applauding! Here the Jets were their rivals but the fans were happy for the AFL. It was a big moment in New York, because the old Titans had never been able to sign anybody before. They had drafted guys but never signed them because Wismer didn't have the money—and now they did! The AFL was stealing picks from the NFL!"

We still had a solid defense in 1966, but Tom Sestak's knee was hurt so much by this time that he couldn't practice. Our offense had a good year, and our rookie running back, Bobby Burnett, gained 1,185 yards and was named AFL Rookie of the Year. Jack Kemp also had a good season. One game of significance was our matchup October 8 against the Denver Broncos. Our old head coach, Lou Saban, after one season at Maryland was now the head coach of a struggling Denver team. We managed to win, 17-16. We ended the year 9-4-1, good enough for first place in the Eastern Division. For the third year in a row, we were going to the championship game.

Nothing hurts more than losing a game, except losing a playoff game or a championship. Back in 1963, we had a playoff against the Boston Patriots, because we'd tied in the Eastern Division. And they beat us to go on into the playoffs. That was a tough one to lose. In 1966, we ended up playing Kansas City for the AFL Championship. We lost that game, of course, 31-7. In truth, we beat ourselves with mistakes as much as Kansas City beat us, but they earned the right to play in the first Super Bowl, against the NFL champion Green Bay Packers. The word in those days was that the AFL wasn't as good as the NFL, that we couldn't compete with them, and so on. So, it was a big letdown that the Bills didn't get the chance to play. Not that Kansas City was a bad team, but it would have been a unique opportunity for us.

I think in some ways we matched up better against Green Bay than Kansas City did. And I like to think we could have beaten Green Bay. Green Bay ended up winning, which only "proved" to a lot of people that the NFL was superior. I know Packers coach Vince Lombardi was certain that the Bills were going to win the AFL Championship. I think he was relieved when the Chiefs beat us, because he knew he matched up better against Kansas City than he did against us.

Was the NFL superior to the AFL? It's hard to say. We did have a lot of players early on who'd been cut by NFL teams. I was one of them. But we also had a lot of very good players, out of Canada, or out of college, that were every bit as good. Some guys will insist the NFL had the better talent. Maybe this was true in 1960, but by the time I was in Buffalo, I think our talent was just as good as that of any NFL team. The game of football, at any level, is an exciting game, and the AFL played an exciting brand of football that became the norm for the NFL after the merger. In some ways, the AFL was way ahead of the NFL. Lots of passing, flashy uniforms, two-point conversions, better television coverage.

The AFL not only allowed a lot more people to play football, but it also increased the number of fans who could watch it. The AFL got bigger and bigger, and finally landed a network television contract. We all knew we could do it. I played nine years in the AFL and nine years in the NFL. Every year football got bigger and bigger.

I really would have liked to have played in that first Super Bowl. Losing the AFL Championship in 1966 and losing Super Bowl VII in 1972 are the two toughest losses of my eighteen-year career.

In 1967, we traded Daryle Lamonica to Oakland, and he came in to Buffalo with the Raiders and beat us. Lamonica ended up being the AFL Player of the Year. He took the Raiders all the way to the AFL/NFL Championship Game the year after we traded him. The Green Bay Packers won that game by a score of 33–14. Meanwhile, we finished the season with a record of 4-10.

We had traded Tom Day the year before for Tom Flores. Day

was the one that always dropped off of the line to play linebacker when we needed him. He was only 250 and could drop back fast when we read the color for a pass. When the Bills traded him they looked at me and said, "You're going to have to play the linebacker." I guess they did not think Dunaway could catch the ball. I was real excited about that.

For the 1968 season, training camp wasn't at the Camelot Motor Inn. We'd moved to Niagara University in Lewiston, New York. We lived on campus, in dorms. Niagara was farther from Buffalo, and the chemical plant nearby smelled terrible.

We had a curfew every night at Niagara, and if you didn't make bed check you were fined by the team. When Saban was coach, players snuck out, but usually the coaches weren't overly strict about checking the actual beds for warm bodies. Collier was stricter. The fine was $500, and they checked your bed. There was a little bar that we used to go hang out at in Lewiston, and one night we stayed too late and realized we needed to get back for bed-check. Our tight end, Paul Costa, had a Corvette, and I had an old Ranchero. We raced back to the camp, with Costa getting a head start. On the way, I got pulled over by the police.

"Do you know how fast you were going?" the patrolman asked me. I said, "No, sir. I was too busy racing to look at my speedometer." He said, "I'm going to have to give you a ticket." I said, "Do what you gotta do, but unless it's a five-hundred-dollar ticket, I'm gone!" The policeman figured out we were trying to beat curfew, and laughed.

The year 1968 saw another disappointing season. It started out with the Bills drafting an excellent young wide receiver, Haven Moses, out of San Diego State. Thirteen of our draft picks played in 1968. But the expansion draft hurt us. The NFL's new team, the Cincinnati Bengals, picked up five of our players, including our excellent running back and former rookie of the year, Bobby Burnett.

In our second exhibition game, we lost guard Joe O'Donnell to a knee injury, and he was replaced by a rookie, Bob Kalsu, out of the University of Oklahoma. Kalsu was small but very fast. Also in preseason, I got blocked into Jack Kemp's leg in a scrimmage, tearing his medial collateral ligament and ending his season. That left us with our backup quarterback, the rookie Dan Darragh out of William & Mary. In the opener, our starting offense had six rookies. After two losses, Coach Joe Collier was fired. Ralph Wilson replaced Collier with the chief of personnel, Harvey Johnson. One day Ralph walked in and said, "Harvey, you are now the head coach."

Harvey was our scout and had experience as a player and coach. He was Ralph's right-hand man; whatever Ralph wanted, he did. Eventually, wide receiver Ed Rutkowski became our quarterback. We finished the year with a record of 1-12-1. Our defense had more veterans, and was more stable that year, but it wasn't much help. On a personal note, I now had 6 career interceptions, which isn't bad for left defensive end!

Harvey hung on and finished the season, after which he quit. With our terrible 1-12-1 record, we'd get the first draft pick in the upcoming 1969 college draft. The Bills picked O.J. Simpson, the star running back from the University of Southern California.

1. The McDoles at the family farm in Ohio: Charles, Ruth, Ron, Bert, Jackie, Janice, Richard, and Debbie. Courtesy of the Wood family.

2. Ron during his sophomore year at DeVillbis High School, Toledo, Ohio. Courtesy of the McDole family.

3. Ron at the University of Nebraska, 1959. Courtesy of the McDole family.

4. (*opposite top*) 1958 Huskers No. 80, Mike Eger, and No. 88, Ron McDole. Courtesy of the McDole family.

5. (*opposite bottom*) 1959 Huskers No.78, Ron McDole, No. 17, Joe Rutigliano, No. 51, Mick Tingelhoff, and No. 55, Darrell Cooper. Courtesy of the McDole family.

WESTERN UNION

TELEGRAM

W. P. MARSHALL, PRESIDENT

CLASS OF SERVICE
This is a fast message unless its deferred character is indicated by the proper symbol.

SYMBOLS
DL=Day Letter
NL=Night Letter
LT=International Letter Telegram

1201

The filing time shown in the date line on domestic telegrams is STANDARD TIME at point of origin. Time of receipt is STANDARD TIME at point of destination

KA035 0A068

1960 DEC 13 AM 7 36

O PKA051 PKZ1 NL PD=PALOALTO CALIF 12=

SENDER WAITING
Answer
by wire

ROLAND MCDOLE ATHLETIC DEPT=

NEBRASKA UNIV LINCOLN NEBR=

GREEN BAY INTERESTED IN YOU AS DRAFT SELECTION.

1. HAVE YOU SIGNED WITH ANY CANADIAN OR AMERICAN
LEAGUE TEAMS?

2. WILL YOU WAIT FOR N F L SELECTIONS?

3. ARE YOU INTERESTED IN PLAYING FOR PACKERS IF
SELECTED?

ADVISE IMMEDIATELY COLLECT WIRE=

COACH VINCE LOMBARDI GREEN BAY PACKERS GREEN
BAY WISC.

THE COMPANY WILL APPRECIATE SUGGESTIONS FROM ITS PATRONS CONCERNING ITS SERVICE

6. Telegram from Green Bay coach Vince Lombardi letting Ron know they were interested in drafting him. Courtesy of the McDole family.

Green Bay Packers

349 SOUTH WASHINGTON STREET • GREEN BAY, WISCONSIN

BUSINESS OFFICE HEmlock 2-4871
TICKET OFFICE HEmlock 5-4466

Dear Sir:

We are in the process of compiling information on
professional prospects for our 1961 draft and consider you an excellent prospect.

The only way that we can get the complete information
on you, is by your filling out the enclosed questionnaire.

If you entered college or a junior college in 1957 or
prior, you are eligible to be drafted by a professional
team. It is the policy of the Green Bay Packers not
to negotiate with a boy until his remaining collegiate
eligibility is completed.

Please return the completed questionnaire to our office
in the enclosed, self-addressed envelope.

Thank you for your interest.

Sincerely yours,

Vince Lombardi

Vince Lombardi
Head Coach & General Manager

VL/jm
Encls.

1929 1930 1931 1936 1939 1944

MEMBER CLUB NATIONAL CONFERENCE   •   NATIONAL FOOTBALL LEAGUE

SIX TIMES WORLD CHAMPIONS

7. Letter from Vince Lombardi, coach
of the Green Bay Packers, of their
interest in Ron for the 1961 NFL draft.
Courtesy of the McDole family.

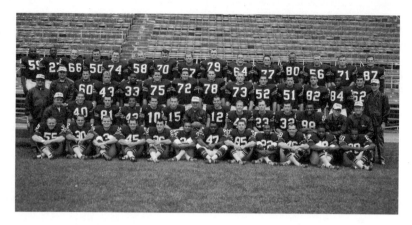

8. 1965 AFL Champions Buffalo Bills team photo. Photo by Robert L. Smith.

9. Bills defense putting the pressure on the Jets' Joe Namath, with Ron getting to him first. Photo by Robert L. Smith.

10. The Buffalo Bills Defense! No. 51, John Tracey, No. 72, Ron McDole, No. 78, Jim Dunaway, No. 70, Tom Sestak, No. 88, Tom Day, No. 58, Mike Stratton, and No. 42, Butch Byrd. Photo by Robert L. Smith.

11. Ron recovering the football and running for the touchdown against Denver, with No. 26, George Saimes, Denver No. 75, Eldon Danenhauer, and Denver No. 2, Cookie Gilchrist. 1965. Photo by Robert L. Smith.

12. Tammy, Taz, and Paula saying
good-bye to Ron at the airport.
Courtesy Buffalo Courier Express.

13. No. 1 fan President Richard Nixon meets Ron McDole, 1972.
Courtesy of the McDole Family.

14. Tackling NY Giants QB No. 15, Craig Morton, with Washington No. 72,
Diron Talbert. Courtesy of the Washington Redskins.

15. (*opposite top*) Coach George Allen talking to the
defense: No. 55, Chris Hanburger, No. 79, Ron McDole,
No. 48, Jon Jaqua, and No. 29, Ted Vactor. 1971. Courtesy
of the Washington Redskins.

16. (*opposite bottom*) Ron intercepting Cardinal Jim Hart.
Courtesy of the Washington Redskins.

17. (*above*) Washington Redskins Over-the-Hill Gang:
Myron Pottios, Ron McDole, Richie Petitbon, Diron
Talbert, and Jack Pardee. Courtesy of the Washington
Redskins.

18. Ron hosting the annual Bills Halloween party as Super Bug! Courtesy of the McDole family.

19. Ron's family: Taz, Ron, Paula, Tammy, Tracey, and Mick. 1980. Courtesy of the McDole family.

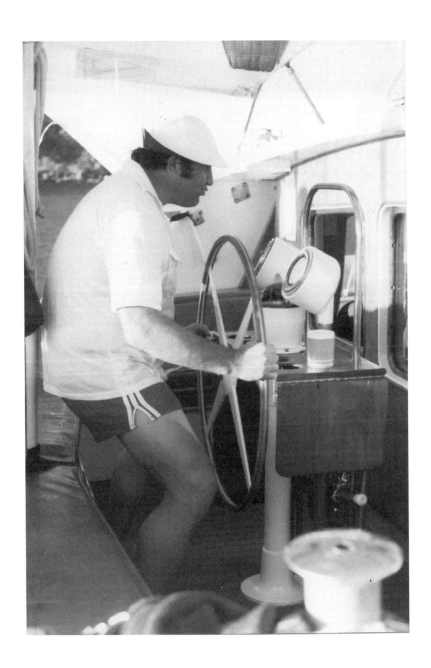

20. Ron pretending to drive the
boat, noises included.
Courtesy of the McDole family.

21. Ron showing off his dance moves
at his niece Andrea's wedding, 1991.
Courtesy of the McDole family.

9
Good-bye, Buffalo

n 1969, I started all fourteen games, and we finished 4-10-0. In 1970, I again started all fourteen games, and we finished with a record of 3-10-1. For the 1969 season, we had a new coach, John Rauch. The Bills had considered George Allen, who had been the head coach for the Los Angeles Rams, and Chuck Noll, the defensive coordinator and backfield coach for the Baltimore Colts, but Coach Rauch, who had been successful coaching the Oakland Raiders, got the job. More on Rauch later. The other big change on the Bills was that we had drafted running back O.J. Simpson out of the University of Southern California. It seems like a small amount now, but O.J. wanted $1 million over ten years, plus a $500,000 loan. Wilson turned him down. O.J. held out. We also selected a black quarterback out of Grambling named James Harris, who became the first black player ever drafted as a quarterback.

On a down note, our 1968 Rookie of the Year, Bob Kalsu, was drafted into the army during the off-season, and one of our quarterbacks, Dan Darragh, was also called up with the National Guard. Kalsu ended up going to Vietnam, and he would be killed in action there.

Rauch had been successful in Oakland, but he was a totally different kind of coach than Lou Saban. Lou saw his players as people, and, as a people person, he could figure out what motivated each player to perform on the field. It was soon obvious that Rauch had a different style and vision altogether. There was going to be a shakeup.

As Booker Edgerson says in Jeff Miller's book *Rockin' the Rockpile*, "it was like a bad dream. He was the worst coach I ever had. The guy was terrible. I think he went on the success of Al Davis—it wasn't him. He came in here with all his philosophy. . . . It was just a mess. As soon as he saw somebody having fun, he'd stop it."

Other players on the 1969–70 Bills use similar language. Charley Ferguson says 1969 was the year he hated playing football. "[Rauch] made football miserable," he recounted in *Rockin' the Rockpile*. "That was the only time I hated to be on the football field and practice. He was just nasty."

Center and long-snapper Howard Kindig played on the Bills. He told me a few years back, "Ron and I played together for five years in Buffalo. I missed the glory years in Buffalo. We had five coaches in the time I was there—Collier, Johnson, Rauch, Johnson again, and Lou Saban in '72. In 1970, the Bills had a terrible year. We won one game that year. We had a tackle get hurt, and so I played some tackle as well. Even though we were a poor team, Ron always gave 100 percent hustle on the field. It didn't matter what the score or what our record was—he gave all he had."

"I was lucky," said Howard. "I planned to retire after the 1971 season, but Don Shula traded for me in the off-season. When he called, I told him my plans to retire and said I wasn't in shape. 'I'll get you in shape,' Shula told me. So I went to Miami, and that year we went undefeated and won the Super Bowl. Quite a turnaround from the last few years in Buffalo."

We hadn't had a very good football team for a few years at this point, but the defense was still strong. Rauch, however, wanted to change the defense, too. Rauch wanted to take me out of pursuit, and that had always been my strength. Our D-line coach told Rauch that the only way he could take me out of pursuit was by cutting my head off. Rauch ignored him.

Rauch didn't realize he had some very smart players on his defense—guys who could be coaching. We were older, some of

us already in our thirties. I was thirty in 1969 and had been playing pro football for eight years. I knew the game and how to play
my position, and suddenly I have a coach who is trying to get me
to do things that go against my playing instincts and my work
experience.

Mike Stratton remembers, "When the Rauch era started, we all
watched Ron, wondering, 'Is Ron able to change to our new "system," where he can follow the ball but not pursue down the line?'
The coaches asked a lot of players, myself included. We all said
he would not change. When Rauch let him go, Redskins coach
George Allen got a fine player, someone who was not going to quit."

Rauch tried to put in a West Coast offense without having the
players to make it work. He was suspicious and paranoid, closing our practices and treating us like high school kids. Training
camp was closed to protect us from "spies." Bed checks were
strictly enforced.

After a long holdout, O.J. Simpson finally signed a four-year,
$215,000 contract in August. He didn't really want to play in
Buffalo. Here we were, the worst team in the AFL, and he was a
Heisman Trophy winner. We also signed Marlin Briscoe from Denver. He'd been the first black quarterback to start for an AFL or NFL
team the previous season, and Rauch made him play wide receiver.
During the preseason, George Flint and Tom Sestak retired. The
season was an exercise in frustration. We finished 4-10. It was a
combination of things, the biggest being too much change and a
coach who didn't know how to deal with his players.

That preseason, the Bills also released Ed Rutkowski, a valued teammate for six seasons. Ed played his college ball at Notre
Dame, and was signed by the Buffalo Bills as an undrafted player
in 1963. A versatile athlete, he played for Buffalo as a defensive
back, wide receiver, punt and kickoff returner, and quarterback.
Primarily a wide receiver, he was named to the 1965 AFL All-Star
team. He was active in politics and entertained fans as the color
commentator on Bills radio broadcasts in the seventies.

Ed recalled, "The AFL in the sixties was a lot of fun. You had personal relationships with the fans and with the players. The fans could come to Meet the Bills Night during training camp. They could come right down on the field and take photos, get autographs, and even compete in events against the players. We had contests like field goal kicking–contests or the 40-yard dash. The AFL was absolutely as competitive a league as the NFL. A lot of our talent came from smaller schools. Elbert Dubenion was recruited out of Boston College. At that time, nobody paid much attention to Boston College. Tom Sestak was recruited out of McNeese State, another small school. The AFL's recruitment of quality players from smaller schools led to the expansion of the scouting systems in both the AFL and the NFL.

"There were, at the time, only thirty-five or thirty-six players on a team. We were more of a family. We backed each other up. If someone got hurt, somebody else would play that position, even if it wasn't their main position. We had Halloween parties at Ron and Paula McDole's house in Eden, New York, that were very fun. Ron would dress up in crazy costumes. One year he was a belly dancer. I went one year as a mummy. I got three rolls of tape and some gauze from our trainer Eddie Abramoski. Then I put on a pair of long underwear and wrapped myself up in gauze and tape. At the party, I had to go to the bathroom and I had to run around the house looking for a pair of scissors so I could cut the tape and use the restroom! Those parties united us, and we really were like a family. Yes, some of the black players came dressed as the KKK and burned a cross on the lawn. They knew they could do that because they knew that we would back them up. We could joke with each other, but if anybody else did something like that to insult our black players that was fighting words! We always supported each other. At the end of the game, we would console each other if someone needed it. It did not matter what color the guy's shoulder or hand was—he was our teammate.

"The relationships we started in the fifties and sixties last to this day. We became very close. I stayed close to guys like Booker

Edgerson, Ernie Warlick, and Charlie Ferguson for years after
we stopped playing.

"My last year at Buffalo, in 1968, we had a bad season. Jack
Kemp got hurt, then Dan Darragh and Tom Flores got hurt. Even
our fifth-string quarterback, Kay Stephenson, got hurt. I was a
wide receiver, but I played multiple positions. I played the last
half of the season as the starting quarterback. I hadn't played
quarterback since my freshman year at Notre Dame! The last
game of the season, we played against Oakland, and we had a
chance to win, but I made a mistake on a play, and we lost. That
loss made us the worst team in the AFL that year, 1-12-1. But
it also gave us the first draft pick in the 1969 draft, and we got
O.J. Simpson. Years later, I used to remind owner Ralph Wilson
that by losing that game I'd helped him get O.J. 'I got you O.J.
because we lost!'"

Leading into the season, I had the honor of being interviewed
on the rigors of training camp for the 1969 Buffalo Bills Annual.
The article begins, "Ron McDole knows the sprains and strains,
drills and pills, releases and rewards of training camps stretch-
ing from Bemidji, Minnesota, to Houston, Texas, from Lake Forest, Illinois, to Niagara University, New York.

"I've been to a few," said Buffalo's outstanding defensive end
(a.k.a. me). "Some have been tougher than others. None are
really easy. . . . But overall, there's generally that initial good
feeling about being back playing football again. You just don't
play football, I don't care what anybody says, unless you like the
game. Then, the initial soreness sets in—because you haven't
been playing for several months. No amount of pre-camp running or anything else prepares you for it. Once you're over that,
if you haven't been nicked along the way, you can feel yourself
getting sharper. Reacting better. The rustiness is leaving. Still,
somewhere along the way, boredom seeps in. . . . You begin to
look forward to the preseason games. You can take your frus-
trations out on someone else, you know. Finally, if you're lucky

enough to survive—and I haven't always been—the challenge of the season is ahead and the dog days of training camp behind for another year."

After we got O.J. Simpson, he was insistent that we get a defensive lineman by the name of Al Cowlings, who was also his teammate at USC. He was drafted number two the year after O.J. was. O.J. and Al were good friends. Cowlings was going to try to take my job.

We had to practice outside, and the weather was a bitch. We had to run all the plays that the other team would run that week. Our defensive coach, Ray Malavasi, would run us through them with Al and me taking turns. It was quite a workout. One practice, we showed up for the meeting, and the snow was blowing outside. It was miserable, and there was no Al. I asked Ray, "Where's Al?" Ray said, "He called in sick today. He had the sniffles. He's kinda sick and he doesn't want to go outside." Okay, something else you never do in the AFL or NFL is miss practice. And I said, "What about me? I've been sick for two weeks!" I got to play twice as many plays, and I wasn't happy about that.

In 1970, we got a little worse, finishing 3-10-1. When it comes to Rauch, it was a bad situation. He tried to change the whole damned team overnight—a team that had won back-to-back championships only a few short years before.

I'd spent eight years in Buffalo, and loved it there. I had been with the team through its highs and lows. The year 1964 had been an incredible one. We'd built a very good football team. Playing football was fun. Tom Day and I used to have a saying before plays: "I'll see you in the backfield." I made the AFL All-Pro team in 1965 and 1967. Then we kind of hit the skids for a few seasons.

The year 1970 marked the official beginning of ABC's *Monday Night Football*, and then, as now, the focus was on the showbiz, the glitz, and the announcers. Monday night football had been done before, but not in all caps. This was something new.

The experiment began on September 21, 1970. The Cleveland Browns were playing Broadway Joe and the New York Jets. ABC had won the rights to televise thirteen Monday night games for three years, paying $8.6 million. Cleveland won, 31–21.

Roone Arledge, the brilliant producer who had made AFL games such great spectator events in the early sixties, now prepared to do the same with the new, combined, AFL/NFL of 1970. Arledge had continued to hone his brand of sports broadcasting in the sixties, focusing on human drama and on the individual athlete as much as on athletic event. Nowhere did he do this better than on ABC's Wide World of Sports—where each show began with the words "the human drama of athletic competition."

Arledge mixed up a potent alchemy in the announcer's booth as well, throwing traditional sportscaster Keith Jackson together with aw-shucks former Dallas Cowboy "Dandy Don" Meredith and one of the most unlikely superstars of the seventies, a pompous, opinionated, toupee'd windbag named Howard Cosell. An American cultural phenomenon was born. And it's still going strong all these years later.

Just prior to the season on July 21, 1970, Buffalo's 1968 Rookie of the Year, Bob Kalsu, was killed in Thua Thien-Hue Province, South Vietnam, becoming the only American professional athlete to die there. Kalsu was an All-American offensive lineman out of Oklahoma, drafted in the eighth round with an eye to the future of the Bills' O-line. Billy Shaw loved him. He loved the way Kalsu had quick feet, and how fast he was on sweeps, great on traps, because at that time Buffalo was primarily a running team. Billy figured that Bob would replace him when Billy retired. He was big, 6 feet 3 inches and 240 pounds, and he was quick. After Joe O'Donnell was injured, Kalsu stepped right in and played excellent ball for nine games. Kalsu was a quiet guy who let his actions on the field speak for him.

Bob was called to active duty in March 1969 and commissioned a lieutenant. While other players got deferments, Kalsu honored his ROTC commitment. He didn't show up at training camp that summer in 1969, missing the entire 1969 season, and arrived in Vietnam that November. Kalsu was standing outside of his bunker reading a letter from his wife when he was killed by an incoming round. He had a wife and a child, and a second child was born two days after Bob was killed. Billy Shaw says that "no one will ever know how great a football player Bob may have been, but we do know how great a man he was to give up his life for his country."

In the 1971 off-season, somebody I knew said I'd been traded to Washington. I went to Coach Rauch, who was paranoid as hell and trying to change everything in Buffalo. We were having a disastrous season. Jim Dunaway and I went to Rauch and said, "Let's bury the hatchet." I thought after our conversation that it was all taken care of. I left the meeting feeling good. When I found out that Rauch wanted to trade me, it all changed. Everything got nasty.

As Ed Abramoski told me in 2014, "when John Rauch became the coach, Rauch wouldn't let Ronnie pursue. Ronnie didn't like to play for Rauch. He took all his stuff out of his locker one day, and took it all home. Ten days later, he brought all his stuff back to the locker room and started putting it all back in his locker."

"It's all going to be okay," he told me. "Rauch says we'll work it out." That same night, on the six o'clock news, they said, "Ron McDole has been traded to the Redskins. I could not believe it. Ronnie was never hurt. He was a great player.

"Lou Saban knew what to do as a coach. Rauch didn't. Rauch tried to make O.J. Simpson into a wide receiver, a punt returner, and a kickoff returner. When Lou got rehired, he called O.J. into his office and asked, "Are you ready to carry the ball thirty times a game?" And we all know how that turned out.

Rauch had a coach's show on TV. He went on his show and bad-mouthed me, saying I had not lived up to past performances and was not playing up to my potential and that he wanted to trade me. I was thirty-two years old. I'd led the team in tackles, inter-

ceptions, and other categories, so I felt his criticism was unde-
served. Then he trashed George Saimes and Paul Maguire the
same way. The whole town of Buffalo was ticked off about it. Buffalo fans are great people, and they understand the game and the
players. I'd run into fans every day at the store, and they'd always
tell you if you did well or poorly. I loved that. Bills fans were really
truthful. The fans raised hell about Rauch's comments.

On May 11, 1971, I was traded to the Washington Redskins for
third- and fourth-round draft picks.

The fact that I had not played what Rauch called "winning football" for the last three years was news to me. I'd led the defensive line in tackles in 1970. Now I was hearing that I was washed
up. I never publicly addressed Rauch's comments, but the fans
in Buffalo were furious. Rauch tried to say he was just defending Ralph Wilson, who'd made the trade.

My second year in Washington, around the time we reported
to the Redskins' training camp, Ralph called me up on the phone.
He told me that after Rauch bad-mouthed me on that show, Wilson got so many letters and calls from people in Buffalo, it was
unbelievable. He told me, "I had a pile of stuff on my desk. And
everybody was criticizing me for not standing up for you, and
Paul Maguire, and George Saimes. Even the people in my own
front office, people who are your friends, told me that I couldn't
just let this situation go. I'm still getting letters and comments
from fans. It hasn't stopped. This happened a year ago! And now
we can't compete because Rauch let all his players go!"

A few years later, I ran into him at one of the Bills alumni functions. He always came to these functions, even though he lived
in Detroit. He especially liked us older guys, since we were the
ones who made him a success.

Ralph explained, "I want to tell you, I did not want to trade you.
George Allen, the new Redskins coach, would call me at two or
three o'clock in the morning trying to make a trade for you and I
felt you were one of our better players, one of our captains along

with Jack Kemp. And George Allen was driving me crazy. After I got to thinking about it, I figured we were going to be drafting a lot of new guys, and I okayed the trade even though I didn't want to lose you because I thought it would be the best thing for you.

"I really didn't know what to do. Finally, I called John and said I wanted to see him in about an hour at the practice area. Then I got in my car and went out to Niagara where the team was practicing. I really didn't know what I was going to do. But I knew I had to do something. I was really pissed. Rauch had a five-year contract.

"I call him in and told him we had a problem. 'What's that?' he asked. I told him, 'I'm going to leave here, and I'm going to drive back into town, and I'm going to talk to the press, because the press is demanding something from the ballclub. I saw that program you did on television, where you criticized McDole and the others, especially your bad-mouthing of McDole, who was our team captain, and whom you said wasn't playing up to his former abilities. Ron McDole has made more tackles in the last five years than anybody on the team. You had no authority to make those comments, John.'

"'Then I quit,' Rauch said. I said, 'Good! I want your resignation on my desk in an hour!' and walked out. I didn't give him chance to renege or anything. I was so goddamned happy at that moment! I'd wanted to fire him so many times. And I even bought him out of his contract."

In the end, John Rauch didn't fire me. I fired him. I always did appreciate Ralph coming up to me and telling me that.

My trade to the Redskins was the best thing that ever could have happened to me at that point in my life. I never thought I'd have another situation like the one I'd enjoyed in Buffalo. The Skins were different. Now I was going to a team that was *not* young. In fact, I was going to a team with old people. They *wanted* old people. Jack Kemp had already run for office and gone to Capitol Hill representing the Buffalo suburbs, and when we got together we used to joke that Washington was kind of like the old folks' home. We were a bunch of guys who knew football, and we had a coach who really knew football. And a few years later, we got to go to the Super Bowl. The Redskins also went to the playoffs four or five years in a row, and we had great success. For me, it was like hanging out at the retirement home. There were all these other players, about my age, thirty-some years old.

A final comment on statistics. Many of the old-school guys had great stats that were never recorded. The leagues didn't start keeping stats consistently until after the older players were retired. They did not keep a tally of sacks. Hell, Deacon Jones must have had one hundred more than they ever said he did. They did not keep these records, and now the record books are cheating all the older guys, including me. Gosh, I do not know how many fumbles I had, 17, 18, 19? And they did not keep track of blocked extra points or field goals. It's just a shame for all those players who will not get the credit due them.

10

The Over-the-Hill Gang Is Born

When I first got traded from Buffalo to the Washington Redskins, I didn't know what to expect down there. My friend Jack Kemp, our former quarterback on the Bills, had been elected to Congress, and he filled me in on the area, mentioned some things to me about the city and stuff like that. I thought Washington would be a political town, which it was, but I also thought that the Washington fans would not be the same type of fans as the ones we had in Buffalo. I figured the Washington fans would be standoffish, and not nearly as dedicated as the Bills' fans. The people in Buffalo were so involved. I'd go into a drugstore or a grocery store and I knew that the little old lady behind the counter would chew me out if I'd missed a tackle or got blocked on a big play, because Buffalo fans knew everything about the game. They knew who was pulling, who was trapped, who screwed things up. In Washington, I didn't think it would be anything like that. Well . . . it was. The Washington fans were just as knowledgeable, and they knew what was going on. Maybe they drove nicer cars than the fans up in Buffalo, but they were great fans. I never expected that.

Right after I got traded, my phone rang. It was early in July, and I was getting ready to take my kids on our big annual Canadian fishing trip. It was George's secretary. "Coach Allen would like to speak to you," she said, and she put him on. "What are you doing?" George asked. I said, "I'm getting ready to go fishing."

"What?!" George was flabbergasted. "It's time to get going! Who goes fishing?!" George finally relented and agreed to let me make the trip. But when I got back, in mid-July, there was a plane ticket waiting for me and instructions to report to the Redskins' DC offices on K Street. It was still only mid-July.

I went downtown and started talking to a couple of the coaches. George Allen came in and he was all excited as he welcomed me into his office. "It's great! We're going to do this and that!" He looked me in the eyes and said, "Well, Ron, how does it feel to be on a winner?" The funny thing was, the Redskins had been as bad as the Bills for years and we had crushed the Redskins the year before in my last year in Buffalo. But that was how he opened. That's how confident he was.

He introduced me to one of the coaches, Torgy Torgeson, and some of the other coaches and staff in the office. We started watching game film from the previous season. The defense looked terrible. George watched the film, and suddenly stopped it and looked at me. "Now do you know why you're here?" George Allen was always all about defense. He thinks the offense is just out there to give the defense a rest! He ran the defense and let other coaches worry about the offense.

George took us down to Georgetown University, where some of the local guys who lived in the DC area during the off-season were working out. "Torgy will take you down there and show you around," he told me. We drove over and I changed into workout gear. The coaches were timing people, and people were exercising and working out. But Torgy just followed me around, answering all my questions, being a very nice guy. There was a huge scale that he made sure we walked by many times, but I never got on it, and never even thought about it. I asked him whether he wanted me to get timed, and he said no. It was a bit strange they did not want me to get timed, or work out. We just walked around the facility, and past the scale a few more times, and that was it. About four years later, I was talking to Torgy and he turned to me and said, "I have to tell you something that's been bugging me. I've always wanted to tell you. The last thing George said to me when you got here was, 'Get Ron on a scale and find out how much he weighs.'" Supposedly, I weighed three hundred and some pounds, and George wanted to get confirmation.

"That's why I was following you around that first day," Torgy told me, "and I finally decided that I was not going to embarrass you or insult you by asking you to weigh yourself. Heck, we just paid two draft choices for you. When I got back and George wanted to know how much you weighed, I said, 'George, we just gave two draft picks for this guy and you want to know how much he weighs? If he can't play because he is too heavy, he wouldn't be here in the first place!' George said, 'Yeah, I guess you're right.'"

George began his career as an assistant coach for George Halas's Bears, but had been hired by Dan Reeves to coach the Los Angeles Rams in 1966. Halas accused Allen of negotiating with other teams while under contract, took him to court, and won, but then let Allen go. Halas said of George, "George Allen is a liar. George Allen is a cheat! George Allen is full of chicanery!" That was enough for Vince Lombardi, who told Reeves, "Dan, it sounds like you've just gotten yourself a helluva head coach!"

It was true. George could find loopholes in the rules or circumvent them altogether. Pete Rozelle was usually pissed off at him, as was Howard Cosell. He was also a football genius. He lived, ate, and slept football. He was a helluva good guy to work for, a player's coach. A George Allen defense could have as many as 300 defensive alignments and 150 audibles. We had a huge three-ring binder with hundreds of plays and formations. Often, I'd come home and Paula would quiz me on them. It was complicated, and George knew he needed older, more experienced players to run his system and make it work. He wanted guys on the field who could coach themselves, and call their own plays.

George arrived having been the most successful coach in Rams history. He had a 49-17-4 record in his five-year stay in Los Angeles, and had made the title game twice. He also liked to make trades. When he was fired by the Rams, a lot of teams wanted him, and he was signed by the Skins in about a week. The Redskins were a very old NFL franchise, but hadn't done much for years before the single Lombardi season. The Skins had only had one winning season in the past fifteen, and hadn't been to the play-offs for a quarter of a century!

When George Allen came to Washington, his plan was to pick up all the old players. And the old players were available as hell, and you could get them practically for nothing. But Allen knew that old guys don't make rookie mistakes. He signed a bunch of his old Los Angeles Rams players—some people called those guys the Ramskins. In all, George made nineteen off-season trades involving thirty-three players. Eight of them were former Rams.

One of the "Ramskins" was linebacker Myron Pottios, who arrived from the Rams along with Jack Pardee, Diron Talbert, Maxie Baughan, John Wilbur, and Jeff Jordan. Pottios played twelve seasons and 129 regular-season games in the NFL with the Steelers, Rams, and Redskins between 1961 and 1973, had 12 interceptions and 11 fumble recoveries, and was selected to three Pro Bowl teams as a Steeler.

Mo was tough as hell and he would play up behind us. He was a little short and of course you wanted a taller guy to be a middle linebacker, so he would play up tight on the line a lot.

Mo was in a bar at Tyson's Corner, Virginia, and gave a guy money for the guy's parrot. The guy needed money for drinks. Mo brought the parrot home and his wife threw both him and the bird out of the house. He then brought the bird to our house, because we lived the closest. He tells us, "I have to sell you the bird, I cannot give it away. I got to get rid of the bird. You have kids. Take the bird!" We took on this bird, and that parrot never shut up.

One time when we went from Eden down to Virginia for the football season, we got Joe O'Donnell and his family to watch the bird. When the season was over, we pulled up outside of our house after midnight, in a snowstorm, and Joe walked up to our car with the bird and said, "Here's your bird back!" I'm not sure how he knew we were home but he was there knocking on the door seconds after we got home and said, "Take the bird." I think we gave that bird as a wedding present to someone.

Myron Pottios remembers, "I remember when Ron was traded to the Redskins. We knew he was a veteran player and that he had played in the American Football League. I'd never heard much about the AFL and had never heard much about Ron, but I knew he was nearly a ten-year veteran who had been drafted in 1961, the same as me. I'd gone to the Pittsburgh Steelers, played linebacker there for five years, then gone to the Los Angeles Rams in 1966 when George Allen picked me up. I played for George Allen for five years as a Ram, and I was one of the 'Ramskins' who George brought to the Redskins when he got the head coaching job. The main Ramskins on defense were Jack Pardee, Diron Talbert, and myself.

"When Ron was traded to the Redskins from Buffalo, he came onto the Skins and, once he learned the schemes, he was a perfect fit on our team, not only on the field but off. He was a great asset to our defense. Though Ron never had the chiseled, muscled body of a Deacon Jones or a Bruce Smith, he was very quick, much quicker than he looked. He had quick feet and quick hands. And he was smart. Instead of taking a hit head-on, he was quick enough to side-step. He had amazing longevity as a player. Ron was never hurt! He was just so consistent.

"When he showed up in camp from the Bills, Ron quickly proved himself that he could play. Not only could he play, but he had the ability to fit in with the guys already on the team, not only the old-time Redskins like Chris Hanburger but also all the Ramskins. Ron is a happy-go-lucky guy. He's always smiling and always positive. I've never seen him ever when he was not happy, and never seen him negative. To me, his greatest ability was his ability to fit into the team almost from the first day, and play at a high level for many years.

"When you looked at Ron, you might ask yourself, 'How the

hell does he do it?' He is the epitome of the saying, 'You cannot tell by looks.' Ron's body type was deceptive to his speed and agility. And it wasn't that he didn't have muscle! You don't hit as hard as Ron did without having plenty of muscle!

"The fact that Ron could play eighteen years as a pro tells you a lot about his talent. In pro sports, if you don't produce, you're gone. They have all your plays on film. They can look very carefully, and if you don't play at a high level, you're gone. When a player gets to a certain age, you know it's just a matter of time, and that your time is coming. Ron's ability to play eighteen years speaks to his talent."

Among my teammates were good, experienced players such as Diron Talbert, Myron Pottios, and John Wilbur. George already had Jack Pardee, who was our defensive general. To wheel and deal for additional experienced players, he got the NFL to extend the trading deadline so he could go after the AFL players as well. That's when he picked up Verlon Biggs and Jimmie Jones from the Jets and me from Buffalo. Verlon and I became the bookends on George's refurbished defensive line. In 1970, I was thirty-one years old. Verlon was twenty-eight.

Another Redskins old-timer was Mike Bragg. He'd been with the Skins during the lean years, in the late sixties, and then with Lombardi, so he'd been around for a while. As Mike remembers it, he and I first met at Georgetown University Field House in the spring of 1971. Mike said, "He [Ron] was wearing bib overalls, and I was thinking, 'How can he still be playing?' Well, he soon demonstrated to me that you can't judge a book by looking at the cover! On the field he had great athletic ability, great feet, and great balance. Blockers couldn't get him off his feet, hence the name 'Dancing Bear,' although some claim that moniker could have come from certain dance floors on M Street in Washington DC. I was always amazed at why teams even tried to run wide to his side, their right side, his left. Running to Ron's side, with Jack Pardee and Pat Fischer right behind him, was not a good choice for opposing teams. Even though most teams are right-handed. That was not a good route!

"Ron, or 'Dole,' as we called him, was a great field goal blocker, too. He said that what he would do was puff himself up similar to what a horse does when you saddle it, and then when the ball was snapped, he charged into a gap and then exhaled all the air he'd taken in. This made him smaller and he would fit himself through that gap and block that kick!

"We had so many new faces in 1971. All of them were great guys just like Ron. People with character. Solid citizens. We had great times on and off the field in those years. Ron was a true professional and an unspoken low-key leader who could be counted on when you needed a big play. No speeches. No jumping up and down in self-adulation. Just doing his job!"

When George got to Washington, he already had Sonny Jurgensen at quarterback, and Sonny and he were at odds on how to run the game. George was more conservative than Sonny. George hated to pass. Too many things can happen to the ball when it's in the air. "There are too many guys running around back there trying to intercept the ball!" he'd say. He always said if we could run the ball, we would be hard to beat. He said he'd be happy if we won every game 7–0. Sonny had made his reputation by throwing the football. George tolerated Sonny. But Sonny just couldn't stay healthy. Sonny got hurt the last exhibition game, and he played through the year off and on.

Sonny was a great football player, and I would have played with him anywhere. He's the one who attached the name "The Dancing Bear" on me. He was nearing the end of his career when we played together. I remember Sonny's accurate passing. Recently, he was kind of enough to share his memory of me. "Ron McDole is a special person, and he was a special player," Sonny said. "He had such very quick feet. He was almost impossible to block. Some guys have quick hands. Ron had quick feet." Well, he did nickname me "The Dancing Bear."

Sonny was used to being the Redskins' number-one quarterback, and then we made that trade for Kilmer with the Saints because George wanted someone who was capable of backing up Sonny. That kind of started the whole Sonny/Billy debate. The thing was, we had two quarterbacks. One was a natural, outstanding, Hall of Fame passer. That was Sonny. The other could also throw the ball, but he relied on other things, and used the running game. That was Billy. On defense, we really didn't care who the quarterback was. We were going to play defense no matter what. George just wanted us to keep people from scoring, and he would be happy only if no one scored on us. The offense did what they had to do to give us some time off the field, but that did not happen very often.

George told me once, "You know, people laughed at me when I traded for Billy Kilmer, right at the last minute, right before the season started." George brought Kilmer onto the Skins in 1971. A lot of people thought that Billy was just a journeyman quarterback by this point in his career. Billy had been an outstanding player at UCLA, and contrary to what most Skins fans believe, at one time he was a great scrambling quarterback. In fact, his first year in the pros, in 1961, he was used primarily as a running back. He rushed for 509 yards and 10 touchdowns.

In 1962, Billy was in a serious car accident in San Francisco. He almost lost his foot. His legs were crushed, and people thought his career was over, but Billy worked his way back into football. He sat out the 1963 season, and played only a little on the Niners after coming back in 1964.

When the NFL awarded a franchise to New Orleans, Billy went to the Saints in the expansion draft. He played some great games, but saw the writing on the wall with the arrival of quarterback Archie Manning, and asked the Saints to trade him. George picked Billy up for a linebacker and two draft picks, intending for Billy to back up Sonny. Sonny threw a beautiful tight spiral, and Billy's passes tended to wobble a bit on their way to the target, but he was accurate.

Billy Kilmer truly saved the 1971 season for us. He had an excellent season. Billy Kilmer is one of the most courageous players I've played with or against. He played hurt as well as anybody I've ever seen. Lots of people play hurt, so long as their effort doesn't hurt the team. But even so, Billy stood out. I watched him from the sideline. One year we were trying to get into the playoffs and he was suffering from diverticulosis, and during the week he was in the hospital and then on the weekends he checked out to play. He did that for two games. He could play hurt. He may not always have looked pretty, but he could play. He'd play and get the job done. And anybody who played with him during his Redskins years admired him.

When Sonny tore his Achilles at Miami in the last exhibition game, Billy was right there ready to go.

Someone once described George Allen as being so square you could roll him on a Las Vegas craps table. He didn't drink, smoke, or swear. His favorite drink was milk. His favorite movie was *The Sound of Music*. But George understood that we were older, experienced players, and he gave us the leeway to have fun on the team.

For example, Diron Talbert always had great hats for everybody. He'd hand them out and we'd wear them on the sidelines and at practice. Later, companies would send us free boxes of hats, because we wore these crazy hats on the sideline. Pardee had a polka-dot one, Talbert had a psychedelic one, Pottios wore an engineer-style painter's cap. Nobody liked us wearing those crazy hats on the sideline. Pete Rozelle hated them. George Allen didn't care. He cared only that we played good football. He also didn't care whether we had long hair or sideburns. "Short hair doesn't make you a solid citizen," he said. "I respect the player and what he does on the field more than what his hair looks like."

With George, we were the old guys, the solid citizens, the guys he knew he could count on, and he was just keeping us alive. We could outsmart people. We were all knowledgeable. It was like having a bunch of coaches out on the field. We already know how to execute the plays. With our experienced defense, a coach could sit over on the bench and smoke a cigarette and not do anything, and you would get a decent game.

Our defense, called all our own plays on the field. We'd go over everything during the week, but we already knew it, and it was just a matter of knowing when to call what play or formation. George didn't call the plays. We did. Now, we would follow his philosophy for that game, especially the middle linebacker, the captain of the defense, who was normally Jack Pardee, and later Chris Hanburger.

Chris Hanburger played outside linebacker on the Washington Redskins from 1965 until 1978. Considered one of the greatest outside linebackers to ever play the game, he was a nine-time All-Pro. He is one of the 70 Greatest Redskins as well as being in the Hall of Fame in Canton, Ohio. An ironman, he once played 135 straight games.

Chris recounted, "There are a few stories that I'll never forget. One is the story of Ron's dog, J.J., and his daughter Tammy's cat, Sam. I assume this is a true story—you'll have to check with Ron. The family had a dog when they lived up in the Buffalo area in a big house that had been an old brewery. It was a Basenji, which is a South African dog that doesn't bark. It was wintertime. Somehow, this dog had gotten loose while Ron was at practice. When he got home, he found the dog had somehow hung himself from a tree. Ron knew he had to get it down before the kids saw it, so he climbed up and got it down, and then dug a hole and buried the dog. However, the ground was so frozen he couldn't dig very deep.

"The family also had a cat, Sam, who was very close to that dog. When Ron got home the next day, there was the dog, propped up against one of the walls in the sheltered entryway to the house. The cat had dug him up and brought the dog home again.

"Ron put the dog in a plastic bag and put him in the freezer until spring."

(Author's note: Tammy McDole confirms this story, adding that the cat dug the dog up not once but twice. The second time, he left the dog next to the road where the kids got on and off the school bus. Then Ron put the dog in the freezer. In the spring, the dog was buried, and Ron covered the body with bricks to prevent another exhumation.)

"Ron was also notorious for finding thong-type underwear and wearing it. Right before bed-check in training camp, he would put on the thong—and nothing else—and cover himself in baby powder. He'd then burst into your room wearing nothing but the thong and a layer of powder, slapping his belly like a sumo wrestler. Then he'd leave. He also did a hell of an elephant imitation, using his arm as a trunk.

"I got fired after the 1978 season. At the end of the year, I met Jack Pardee at his request, and Jack told me he wanted me to come back the next year. But within the next few weeks, I found out I was done. That's just the way it is in the NFL. I got into the Hall of Fame in 2011, as a senior player. I think every player who ever played pro football should get in, but of course they can't do that. There's no way that would work. There's a lot of politicking involved. After I got in, I had representatives for other players contacting me, lobbying me to get their player into the Hall of Fame. I politely declined. Ron would never do that."

George Allen had the philosophy that he didn't like rookies. They make too many mistakes. He figured for every rookie he had in the lineup it cost him at least one game. He preferred veterans who don't make rookie mental mistakes, like jumping off sides, moving early, or fumbling.

All offensive and defensive plays were called from the huddle. George didn't call them. Very rarely he'd send a play in. Billy and Sonny had the same game plan. George was all about the defense, but he knew he could trust his veterans to make good decisions. George worked with Jack Pardee. Assistant Coach Ted

Marchibroda would tell them what to do, but Sonny could do his own thing sometimes.

George Allen was like Lou Saban. He was a people person. He knew how to get his players to give their best. He knew what made each player tick, and to do that, he really had to know his players inside and out. George had an amazing memory.

For example, George had met my family only one time, at a large function, and I have four kids. I took my son Mick to the team dentist in the off-season. It was probably January or February, and Mick had gotten his front teeth knocked out playing hockey. After Mick was done, we stopped by George's office. He was in there, working on plays. George said, "Let me see your teeth." And he said, "Oh, is this Mick?" and he'd never met him before. And then he started talking football, football, football, and I just wanted to get out of there because I knew I'd get enough of that when the season started.

George's coaching philosophy was a lot like Lou's as well. He used to say he could get more done talking quietly one-on-one with a player than yelling. He hated coaches who yelled and screamed, and he would not let his coaches act that way. He would call out a coach for cussing, and I had never been with a coach who did that; it was an unusual thing. George didn't cuss. He never made a big scene. He would deal with a player individually. George always said, "If you don't know how to play football by now, I can't help you."

He had big goals for us as a defense that first year. He wrote the goals into our big, thick playbooks we had to learn. The defense was expected to intercept at least 24 passes and return them for at least 360 yards. He wanted 50 sacks. He wanted 4 defensive touchdowns and for our defense to hold our opponents to 200 points or less. He also had high goals for his special teams. George was a big believer in the importance of special teams. He was the first NFL coach to hire a special teams coach, Marv Levy. He wanted a 24-yard return average, 8 turnovers, at least 4 blocked punts and as many blocked field goals, and so on.

There were a couple of things about George that you needed to be careful about. One was that he'd keep you on the field for a long, long time. Two was that he would talk you to death. He never talked about anything but football. One day, I stopped by his office, and there was a special projector on his table. George was very excited. "Look at that!" he said. It was a new type of projector. "Isn't this great!? Now I can watch four more cans of film every day!" That's how committed he was. Most of us hated watching film. George loved it.

He was like a walking computer, too. He loved every sport and he knew all the statistics. He knew all the baseball batting averages. His energy was unbelievable.

George Allen did not tolerate his players being late or missing meetings or practices. He used to tell me, "If you get in a wreck on the way to practice, you better either die or be on time!" I was always fifteen minutes early. You didn't call in sick in those days. If you were sick, the team doctor could fix it. Or your adrenaline got pumping and you didn't notice. I got cleated in my leg once, blood was pouring out, and I didn't even notice till later. If you wanted to stay around, you'd better be there every day, ready to go. There were too many other guys there that were ready to do your job if you didn't play.

I never missed a ball game until the end of my career. George used to insist we tape our ankles. I have weak ankles, but I hate taping them. It makes me feel restricted in my movements. My ankles are weak and they roll, but I didn't like the stiffness of the tape. But George said we had to tape our ankles, so I'd go get taped with stretchy elastic tape and then have the trainer cover that very, very lightly with tape, just cosmetic really, and it got me by.

He never let us have water during practices. He finally had to because it became a league rule. And he never let us leave the field when there was thunder and lightning. Then we picked up Ken Houston. The first time lightning struck, Ken hustled off the field. Allen let everybody else do it from then on. He didn't want to treat any of his players any differently. If Houston was going to leave the field when there was lightning, then everybody could, and from then on, we did.

When he was hired as head coach, George was given complete control of the team by the Redskins ownership. He was given the NFL's highest coaching salary, a contract packed with perks and incentives, and carte blanche for building the Redskins into a winner. One of the first things he did was drop $500,000 for a new state-of-the-art training facility that would become known as Redskins Park. Before the 1971 season, Redskins president Edward Bennett Williams quipped, "When coach Allen came to Washington, we agreed he had an unlimited budget. He's already exceeded it."

When Allen had come with his Rams to play the Skins in 1969, he'd been shocked at how second-rate the Redskins' practice facilities were. When he requested to build a new practice facility, the owners balked at first. "You want to win or not?" Allen shot back. "You brought me here to win, and this is what it takes. Don't be counting the money!"

The seven-acre facility, also known as "Fort Allen," was built out on the edge of the DC suburbs, about thirty miles from the DC city limits in northern Virginia, next to Washington's Dulles International Airport. The security-conscious Allen built the facility in a wooded area to discourage spying. He also erected a perimeter fence, closed the park off to visitors, and hired a full-time security guard, an old LA policeman nicknamed "Double-O," who doubled as Allen's personal driver, as Allen did not have a driver's license.

Allen's goal was to have the new facility open by the 1971 season, and construction began at once. Two practice fields were constructed—one on grass and one of artificial turf that the team used only before an away turf game. Redskins Park also had a two-story, 22,500-square-foot building equipped with the most up-to-date weight rooms, training rooms, and rooms for team and position meetings and watching film. Redskins Park also had an on-site dentist and a doctor.

George also posted his ten commandments:

Football comes first.

The greatest feeling in life is to take an ordinary job and accomplish something with it.

If you can accept defeat and open your pay envelope without feeling guilty, then you're stealing.

Everyone, the head coach especially, must give 110 percent.

Leisure time is that five or six hours when you sleep at night.

No detail is too small. No task is too small, or too big.

You must accomplish things in life, otherwise you are like the paper on the wall.

A person without problems is dead.

We win and lose as a team.

My prayer is that each man will be allowed to play to the best of his ability.

I found a good place to live not far from Redskins Park, in Reston, Virginia. We rented a house from a tenant who was out of the country. The kids would start school in Virginia that fall. It cost me a lot more money to have a family live in Washington DC than it did to live in Buffalo. I had to maintain our home up in Eden and rent a home for my family to live in in Virginia.

George named me a starter right out of the gate. I became a member of what would become known as the "Over-the-Hill Gang." There were eleven players on the team that year over the age of thirty. Most of us were defensive players, but anybody was eligible so long as he was over thirty and had been released by some other ballclub. Two of the oldest guys were Jack Pardee and Richie Petitbon, who were thirty-five and thirty-three that year. In addition to me, Biggs, Talbert, Pottios, Wilbur, Pardee, and

Petitbon, we also had Bob Grant, wide receiver Roy Jefferson, wide receiver Boyd Dowler, Billy Kilmer and Sonny Jurgensen at quarterback, and Speedy Duncan as a punt and kick returner.

We had a brilliant running back, Larry Brown. He was one of the toughest guys I've ever played with. He ran the ball many, many times a game, and it took a lot of hits to bring him down. He'd be pretty beat-up by the end of the game. He was a quiet leader, a man who leads by his play. Larry ran so hard on every play that everyone respected him. If you are going to be a leader, you must have respect. Larry was also forgiving and realistic about his teammates. I asked him once, after he ran for a long gain that was called back by a holding call, whether he ever got upset because a long run was called back. Larry laughed. "Not really," he said. "There are a lot of times that I miss the hole."

The thing that happened with Larry is he got hurt, and when he hurt his leg, he lost his quickness. What I mean by that is that he could not get off the ball as quickly. It's not something that you notice unless you are a person who watches and under-stands what is happening, but Larry lost something that was so important to him—his explosive running. He was really irritated, and he struggled with it his last year and that really brought him down statistically.

He was a great guy and a team player. He did whatever he had to do to make it all work. He never bitched—he never moaned. I've played a long time and met a lot of runners, and he was one of the finest guys, not only as a ball player but also as a person. He was a great success for the Redskins.

Larry Brown played his entire career for the Redskins, from 1969 to 1976. One of the era's most celebrated rushers, he was a four-time Pro-Bowler, the NFL's Most Valuable Player in 1972, the NFL Offensive Player of the Year in 1972, and the NFC Player of the Year in 1972, led the NFL in rushing yards in 1970, and is one of the 70 Greatest Redskins.

Larry tells this story about me: "One year, Ron was very suc-cessful getting George Allen to put a number of performance

116

bonuses into his contract. One of these was that Ron wanted to be paid for every interception.

"We were playing a team with a formidable running game that season. The team was running the ball easily against us. Ron finally called 'time-out' to discuss the situation with George Allen.

"'What can we do to slow these guys down?' he asked Allen. George said, 'It would help if you would line up on the line of scrimmage instead of in the secondary!'" It's true. I did love getting interceptions.

I was fortunate to never get seriously hurt. I ruptured my bursa sac in my elbow one game, broke some fingers over the years, broke my nose in my first game. But nothing serious. Still, I remember one time I scared Billy Kilmer with getting treatment for an injury. I've played many times sick or hurt. You just play off the excitement of the game, and you run on adrenaline. The mind is an unbelievable thing. One time, I had terrible gout in my toe. I've had gout all my life. And the Skins had some drug that they could shoot into you and knock out the gout. It was used at all the racetracks as a tranquilizer on horses.

One week, the day before a game, we'd have a Saturday practice and then stay at the hotel out at Dulles Airport. I had my shot and expected to feel like a million the next day. I woke up the next morning and I could hardly walk. My toe was killing me. I had to go into this little room for another shot. Billy Kilmer had injured his shoulder the previous week, and he was due in the room as well for a shot in his shoulder. He and I were sitting in the little training room at RFK waiting for the doctor. Soon, the doctor showed up.

The doctor asked, "How's the toe?" I said, "It hurts like a son-of-a-bitch!" The doctor nodded and said, "We're gonna have to shoot this thing. Let me warn you that the injection will be unbelievable and will hurt like crazy."

I have a reputation for having a high pain tolerance, so I said to go ahead and give me the shot. I needed to play. Billy watched from the other table.

"That does *not* look like fun," Billy said. The doctor takes out this huge needle, and to this day, the only time I've felt pain like that was one time at the dentist when the dentist hit a nerve and I went through the roof. Billy was watching me wide-eyed the whole time. Tears started running down my cheeks. Suddenly, no pain. The shot kicked in. Then it was Billy's turn. Billy jumped up off the table. "Goddamn, if you made McDole cry, you ain't *touching* my ass!"

One season a few years later, there was a big controversy over who would start at quarterback for the Skins. Joe Theismann was backing up Kilmer. Well, everybody wanted Theismann and he finally got to start. He ran for his life. He scrambled around and scrambled around and finally George Allen pulled him out and put Billy into the game. They never touched Billy. He knew just how to stay out of reach and stay calm and get things done. Billy was physically and mentally tough. And he was a born leader.

Billy also appreciated his linemen. We had a tradition in Washington that the quarterback would pay for the drinks for the linemen at the Holiday Inn after a game. Billy always bought drinks for his offensive line. Theismann would never pick up a tab for his linemen. Maybe Theismann wouldn't have had to scramble around and would have had better protection if he had picked up the tab.

Billy Kilmer can walk into any room, any place, and be comfortable. Once we went over to Myron Pottios's house in New Orleans. Myron's Ukrainian father didn't speak English, but Billy was totally at ease.

Another great player we picked up was wide receiver Roy Jefferson, whom we called Sweet Pea. Roy was a star on every team he ever played on, including ours. He was also a team player. He would run back from his route and pick Larry Brown up off the grass after a hard tackle. He cared about his teammates. He was a flashy dresser, bright colors and jumpsuits, always dressed impeccably. In his twelve seasons—three of which he made the

Pro Bowl—with the Steelers, Colts (1970 Super Bowl ring), and Skins, Roy had 52 touchdowns, 451 catches, and 7,539 yards.

In 2014, Roy remembered how he made his entrance as a Redskin: "My best Ron McDole story involves my very first appearance at Redskins training camp at Carlisle, Pennsylvania. When the Redskins picked me up, I came to camp from the Colts' camp at Weston, Maryland. I used to dress really flashy, and I danced quite a bit. When I played on the Steelers, Mean Joe Greene, Ben McGee, Ray May, and Chuck Hinton nicknamed me 'Sweet Pea.' There was a sixties song called 'Sweet Pea' with the lines 'Oh, Sweet Pea, come dance with me!' I drove a red Cadillac, with white leather seats and interior and a white vinyl top. I got out of the car wearing a red jumpsuit and white boots. The top of the jumpsuit was down, so no shirt. My arms and chest were out. I was wearing a red tam hat. And I had a brown rawhide leather purse that hung down to my hip. The purse had rawhide strings that hung down to the ground.

"When I got out of the car, the Redskins players were already out on the field practicing. Ron saw me get out and said something to the other players, though I didn't know it at the time.

"Later, we're together at a luncheon where there are about three hundred people, and Ron tells a story. He said, 'When I saw Roy Jefferson get out of the car, I knew George Allen wasn't kidding, man! He'll get us anything we want to win a game. He's gone out and got us a pimp, man!' What's more, he told the story again at a 'Welcome Home' luncheon for about six to seven hundred people after we got home from training camp!"

"On the early seventies Redskins team," Roy continues, "we didn't have the youngest players, but we had a team that did not make a mistake, especially on defense. The defense was always in the right place. If you looked at our guys, as far as looking like athletes, we just didn't have guys who looked athletic. But they could play!

"You had guys like Ron. Ron looked like a fat guy, but he had quick feet and good hands, and he was so smart. And you had guys like Chris Hanburger and Pat Fischer, who were both great players but very small. Bill Brundige was huge, and he was very athletic.

"At first, I didn't like playing for George Allen. We did things over and over again in practice. We went over things twenty times in training. But when game time came, we knew instinctively what we were supposed to do. We'd instinctively know the plays. It was the same with the defense. Instinctive. A lot of teams may have been more athletic, but technically they were not as good as we were. Once I understood what George was doing, then it was fine. He didn't beat us up in practice like some coaches will. We ran practice at full speed but without beating each other up. We ran practice full-speed but we didn't have to hit full speed. I liked that. On other teams, guys would get injured in practice.

"George Allen wasn't sure what to make of me. I wore some crazy outfits in those days. And George used to say, 'We have to leave him alone.' George tolerated the outfits as long as I played well."

Jack Pardee was our defensive field general. He'd also fought hard to play football. Jack found out he had cancer in 1964 but managed to beat it and returned to play with the Los Angeles Rams. When George came to Washington, he brought Pardee with him. Jack had been with George Allen and he was the "General," which is what we called him, and he and George were like one unit. They thought and reacted the same way.

Jack had an almost computer-like football mind. He had lots of experience, read plays very well knew, and always knew what was going on. He was responsible for calling all the plays and all the check offs. We had a very complicated defense, but he would see something and change the call, and everyone would have to shift to the new call from our previous individual changes we'd already made. If you were going to do a stunt on the left or right, and you were all ready to run it, and Jack changed the call, you did not have a choice, you changed to his call. And because Jack read offenses so well, and we could change our plays so quickly, it was very difficult for the offense to block us. Jack knew the game very well and of course went on to be a very successful coach once he left us.

I liked the fact that he was doing all the calling and he was on my side, the left side. Jack was the left linebacker, and he would slip in many times behind me and tap me on one leg or the other leg and that is when he would read the block coming at me. This was a big help to me and helped me to make plays I wouldn't have made otherwise. Jack was really a big help in my career! When Jack left, he was replaced by Dave Robinson, who was a different type of player. Robinson was not a play-caller. So Chris Hanburger became the general after Jack Pardee left, but he really didn't want the job. We used to call him the Grouch. He would grouch about this and that. Chris used to argue with George all the time after George made him the general. He'd say, "I'm not going to watch all those films." George loved watching the films, and our old general, Jack Pardee, wanted to be a head coach, so he was learning everything he could. Chris wanted to play, but he did not want to do anything else other than play. And he was a great player who ran the show. He has mellowed over the years.

George Allen had a saying, and I believe to this day it's true. "Forty men playing together cannot lose!" He built that spirit of togetherness on the Redskins. He was positive and optimistic, and really, really loved the game of football.

In our first home game in 1971, against Houston, I intercepted a screen pass and ran it in 18 yards for a touchdown. That was a great game for me—it was that interception and the fact that I was on a brand-new team in a new city, and it made the fans happy. I was excited—I'd never scored a touchdown. I had about fifteen or twenty yards to go to get into the end zone. By this time, everybody on the field was chasing me.

Verlon Biggs followed me every step of the way on that touchdown, begging for a lateral. Verlon Biggs could have a whole book written about him. What an amazing, funny man, and a great friend. He was a hero in the small Mississippi town he was from. He had a sense of humor where you never knew whether he was being serious or not. Was he telling you the truth or was he lying? Or was he maybe making fun of you? Verlon's locker was next to mine on the Skins. We carpooled from Redskins Park to our houses in Reston. He lived in Cameron Crescent and I lived in Waterview Cluster.

On my interception touchdown against the Oilers, I'd already intercepted the pass and was running for the end zone. I was running about 100 mph and not going anywhere, and Verlon came from the other side of the field, following me while I'm running. He caught up with me 20 yards from the goal line, and he started shouting, "Dole! Dole!"—because he always called me "Dole" rather than "McDole"—"Dole! Dole! Lateral the ball! Lateral the ball! You're not gonna make it!"

And there I was, with guys trying to tackle me and shit, and there was Verlon yelling at me to lateral! I kept looking at him like he was nuts. "Dole, Lateral! Dole, Lateral!"

I *did* make it to the goal line. Everybody piled on top of me, including Verlon. Afterward, Verlon asked, "Hey, you did make it?" I said, "Yeah, and I probably would have made it sooner if you had blocked somebody!" And after the game, Verlon came up to me and said, "Don't let it make you bigger, Dole."

George Allen had a firm rule. "Never pick up a fumble on defense. Fall on it." We were playing in Pittsburgh and Pittsburgh fumbled the ball right toward me, because I'd got inside the tackle. The ball rolled up, I reached down and picked up the ball, and the offensive tackle hit me and I fumbled. George Allen got all over my ass. It killed our momentum and we ended up losing the game. After that, about three times every practice, Verlon would go find a football someplace and while we were waiting for it to be our turn to go in on a drill, he would roll the ball and fall on it and say, "Like this, Dole!"

Verlon had problems with his feet. He had flat feet, and he hated breaking his shoes in. One day, Verlon went into Diron Talbert's locker and took some of Diron's shoes. Diron was off getting taped. I said, "What are you doing, Verlon? Did you forget your shoes?" "No," he said, "my feet are killing me and I need some shoes."

One time I looked over and Verlon had two different kinds of shoes on. He had a Riddell shoe on one foot and a Puma or an Adidas on the other. "What are you doing?" I asked him.

"There's a strategy in this," said Verlon, "Notice that I'm wearing the lighter-weight shoe on the side I need to go around end on. Since that shoe is lighter I'll go around that side of my body faster." I thought he was joking, but he played the whole game with two different types of shoes on.

Verlon would do the strangest things. One game, we were playing the Jets, and Verlon was up against Mighty Joe Young. Verlon had played on the Jets and he knew Young. The game program has photos of all the home team and a few opposing stars. Verlon asked me for my program. I had no idea what he was doing. He took my program and his program and cut out the two little photos of Joe Young. He taped one on his right shoe and one on his left shoe. Right on the toes of his shoes. "Why in the world are you doing that?" I asked him.

He wouldn't say, but he seemed confident in his strategy. Now, normally in a game, Verlon and I crossed each other many times rushing the passer. But the whole first half, I never once saw Verlon. At halftime, we were sitting down, and I looked down at his shoes. One of the photos was all crumpled up and the other was missing completely.

"Verlon, are you playing?" I asked him. "I haven't seen you the whole damned game." It turned out he was, but that Young was manhandling him. Verlon took the little photos off his shoes. His idea had backfired.

Another time we were playing in a charity golf match down in Dallas. Verlon didn't golf. This was a big deal for Dallas Cowboy head coach Tom Landry, a banquet and all, and was after we'd retired. All our expenses were paid to this banquet and tournament, and they needed one more guy to play golf. So Verlon said he would go.

"Verlon, do you play golf?" I asked him. Verlon said, "Sure. I've been playing for years."

I went to the pro and told him Verlon needed a set of clubs. "Are you right-handed or left-handed?" I asked him. "What are you?" asked Verlon. "No, Verlon," I said. "This means what hand do you write with? That's also the hand you hit the ball with." Verlon said that he was right-handed. I gave him three new balls and didn't see him till after the round was done. I waited and waited, and finally I saw him down by a little pond. He looked so beat and tired. I asked for the balls back, and he gave me three old beat-up balls.

"Verlon, those aren't my balls," I told him. "Mine were new." Verlon said, "You're right. Yours all ended up in the woods, the weeds, and the ponds. These will have to take their place."

Verlon had a pet Doberman. It was one tough-looking dog, but that dog got chased home by poodles every day. At his house, Verlon had a big bowl of nuts. One time, I came over to his apartment to pick him up and he was in the backyard around a tree.

"Dole, I got problems." I asked, "What's the problem?" He said, "See my nut bowl? All my nuts are gone. I know it's that squirrel. I see him once in a while and he is eating nuts and I know he's hiding them up in that tree."

The next time I came over, the bowl was full again. "Did you buy more nuts, Verlon?" I asked him. "No, I found them," he said. I asked, "Found them? Where?" "Over there in that tree," said Verlon. "I found out that this squirrel was sneaking into my apartment though a little hole in my screen and stealing my nuts. So, I went out to that tree and climbed up and got them back."

I said, "Don't you feel bad for the squirrel, after all that hard work crawling through your window screen and stealing all those nuts so it can eat for the winter?" "No, that squirrel picked on the wrong house," said Verlon firmly.

Verlon never brought a lunch to practice, but he always seemed to be eating. A typical day at practice would start with a team meeting. Then we'd break down into a defense meeting and an offense meeting. Then we'd take a break and then go to a defensive lineman meeting. This meeting only had six or seven players plus a coach, so it was a small group. I sat in the back with Verlon next to the movie projector. Verlon got up and left a lot. Mainly, he did not want to watch film, but we also found out he was leaving and hunting for food. Diron Talbert had a constant problem with keeping his weight up, and he always had lots of food in his locker. Diron decided Verlon was stealing his food. Diron took a tuna fish sandwich and slathered it with mayonnaise, and then he left it out at his house for two weeks, at room temperature. After two weeks, Diron put the sandwich in a new bag and put it in his locker. A week passed. The sandwich was still there. One day, Verlon got up and left. He was never gone for more than ten minutes. When he got back, he smelled like old tuna fish.

I grabbed Diron and said, "I think we caught your rat!" We went to Diron's locker and the sandwich was gone! "We better warn him! He could get sick!" I said.

"No," said Diron. "We'll wait for him to get sick. Then we'll tell him." But Verlon never got sick. The next year, we came back for mini-camp, and Verlon was already there. We'd had about three days of practice, and after the first day, Verlon got sick. He went to the hospital and straight to the operating room. Appendicitis. When Diron showed up, he was convinced that Verlon had finally eaten that sandwich.

Sadly, Verlon died of cancer. He never told anyone, not even his family. He's buried down in Mississippi, one of the most interesting guys the Redskins ever had.

We won that first home game against Houston 22–13, without a single offensive touchdown. Our kicker, Curt Knight, kicked 5 field goals and an extra point, and I scored the touchdown. With Sonny out, Billy started and he did very well, though some fans didn't like the more conservative offense George had brought in.

That first season, we went 9-4-1. Sonny was injured and didn't play much. Billy took over and led the team. We ran the ball a lot. Larry Brown had almost 1,000 yards rushing, and Charley Harraway had over 600. I had three interceptions and a touchdown. Our defense lived up to George's expectations. We intercepted 29 passes and returned them 480 yards, scoring 5 touchdowns. We recovered 24 fumbles. And we made it to the playoffs. We had to fly west to play the San Francisco 49ers. We lost the playoff, 24–20, but it had been a real turn-around season for the Redskins as a franchise and for many of us as players, and the fans were excited for 1972.

George knew that money was tight for his players, especially us old married guys with kids. We used to joke that we were so poor we had to pool our money to buy beer. It was tough for me, with four kids and two houses to keep up. At the end of my first season in Washington, after we lost the playoff game to San Francisco and the team flew back to Washington, George sent word that he wanted to meet with everybody, to say good-bye before each player left town, and I went in to talk to him. He talked about the game and about what the future would hold for me. I was kind of in a hurry to get going. The car was all packed up and the kids loaded up for the trip back to Buffalo. As I started to walk out the door, he motioned to me and said, "Come here for a minute." I walked back to his desk and he handed me a check for $5,000.

"I know you've been trying to get a little extra money," George said. "And you are well worth it. You had a great season."

I was dumbfounded. "I really appreciate it," I managed to say. "But how can you do this?" "Well," said George, "we can write it off as you doing appearances." I said, "But I don't even live here in the area." George smiled. "I told you it would be easy."

That was the first real bonus I got that was based on performance. The next year, I signed a new contract with George. George negotiated my contract, and I'm sure he negotiated a lot of the other players' contracts, too.

I sat across from him. "Wow," I said. "I finally, after all these years, get to negotiate my own contract. So, do you offer me a contract, or do I have to ask for one?"

"I'll tell you what," he said. "We'll double your salary, right off the top. We'll pay you twice as much as you made last year." That would mean I'd be making $70,000.

I knew what some of the other guys on the team made. We'd talked about it. I'd talked to Diron Talbert, my roommate, about how much he made, and other guys who also played the same position.

I said, "I was thinking maybe something more like $100,000." "Well, that's good," said George. "But I'll tell you what. How about some clauses?" I asked, "What do you mean by clauses?"

"The first one," said George, "has to do with the fact that you weighed 300 and some pounds in Buffalo. I really don't want you weighing that much here. That's *heavy*. We have a weigh-in every Thursday, as you well know. If you stay under 275 pounds, at every weigh-in, all season, I'll give you $15,000." "That's fine," I said. "I accept. We're getting closer."

"Okay, and if you lead the defensive line in tackles, I'll give you $5,000 more. And if you lead in assisted tackles, that's another $5,000." It went on. "If you play 75 percent of the games, without missing a game, I'll give you a bonus for that."

There was more. There were twelve or thirteen incentive clauses in my contract when we got done with it. I got so much for each blocked field goal, and $500 a sack. I never got a whole lot of sacks. The most I got in a year was maybe 9 or 10. That year, it ended up that I was making over $100,000. I was so happy I couldn't believe it. I had no idea I'd get that kind of money.

And that season, I got money for every clause I had in my contract. I ran like a crazy man. I blocked kicks. I intercepted a pass. I did everything I could do. And I tackled like a madman. Do you know how hard it is to weasel down into a pile of bodies and get credit for a tackle? I did it. George mentioned that to me one day. He didn't keep the statistics. "How are you making so many tackles?" he asked. "Easy," I told him. "I just crawl underneath."

The next year, I got all the same clauses back in my contract. Except for new two clauses.

When I negotiate with George that year, I lay out my new clauses. "First, can I change my seat on the airplane?" "What?" says George.

The older guys, whom George referred to as the "Solid Citizens," sit in the front of the plane, where first class is. The coaches like to sit in the back, away from George. George is always sitting in the front row on the right-hand side, with the offensive coordinator, Ted Marchibroda. They're sitting there and going through all the breakdowns for the game. And George is passing play details to me and Richie Petitbon, who are sitting behind him and trying to play gin. I'm a terrible gin player, and I'm usually losing a fortune to Richie. George is passing these papers to me, and I'm passing them to Richie. Believe it or not, that year, I lost $5,000 on all our trips, to Richie Petitbon.

"I'll trade you my sack clause," I propose to George, "if you'll change my seat on the plane." "Change your seat?" asks George. "What's wrong with your seat? You're right behind me, aren't you?" I say, "Yes, but I play gin with Richie and I lost $5,000 to him last year!" He says, "What?! You lost $5,000 playing gin?" "Well, yeah," I say. "But that's for the whole season. Including the playoffs."

He asks, "Why don't you just learn to play gin better?" I say, "How can I focus when you are constantly passing stuff back to Richie to look at?" "Okay," he says, "I'll change your seat. What's the other clause you want?" I say, "I want $5,000 for every interception." I already had 6 or 7 pro interceptions from Buffalo.

To George, a defensive-minded coach, an interception was the biggest thing in the game. He brightened up. "Oh, God, yes!" he says. "Five thousand for every interception. I can go with that."

Shortly after that, before the fourth game of the season, we were out practicing. We'd won our first three games already. George will try to catch you outside. We tried to avoid George, because he'd just talk you to death about football or anything else. And George snuck up and caught up with me while I was standing talking to Diron Talbert waiting for practice to start. Most of the guys would go out and throw the ball around. The old guys would just stand around. We had a bench we could sit on, too, and from there we'd watch everybody warm up before practice. Then we'd go out and practice after warmups. You had to be at least thirty-five to sit on that bench. So, George caught me. I was looking the other way.

"Oh, boy," he said, making me jump. "Isn't it a beautiful day!" "It is, George." He spread his arms out. "Look at these trees! We're off to a great start this year." I nodded. With George, all you had to do was nod. He did the talking.

"And you are off to a heck of a start," he said. "What do you mean?" I asked. He said, "You have three interceptions already in one season." "I know," I said. "That means you're out $15,000." George waved his hand. "Oh, no," he said. "I'm not worried about the $15,000. You just keep getting those interceptions!"

That was my bonus system. It was a lot of fun playing for George, and playing in that organization.

A good coach makes all the difference on a football team. The coach is the key person. It's his offense, his defense, his philosophy. He's the one who picks the people, or at least has a lot to do with it. He knows what he wants to do. He knows the schemes he wants to run. The hardest thing for the coach is to get the right athletes—and enough of them—to play the game and then ensuring that the players carry out his plan for how to run the team. He must set up discipline, what are the dos and don'ts. For example, with George Allen, you knew what you could and couldn't do. And the worst thing you could do was be late. Don't be late.

Most coaches agreed with that. You'd get fined for that, and you could lose your job. It's always interesting when they fire a coach because they say, "Well, I never saw him out on the field playing, so how can it be his fault," but ultimately, it's his fault. The coach is the whole team. I remember George Allen had a statement, "If I could just get everybody ready to play at the same time on the same day!" Now, when I watch I game, you can see players that just aren't ready to play, for whatever reason. It's up to the coach to know what makes every player do his best.

Conversely, a good coach can only do so much with a bad team. He can get you disciplined and get everyone on and off the field, but if you don't have the talent, there's not much you can do about it. It also depends on what makes the team bad. Is it guys who don't pay attention or do you have guys who just aren't good football players? And if a coach can take a bad team and win with it, then the question is moot, because they are no longer a bad team.

The funny thing was, nobody really understood what George was doing at the time. Nobody expected much from a team with so many old players, yet the first year we went to the playoffs, and the next year we went to the Super Bowl. That was a neat, unique group. We all appreciated getting a second chance. I was thirty-two the year we went to the Super Bowl. I'm sure we snuck up on a lot of teams that weren't anticipating us being so good. But George was an amazing individual and an unbelievable coach. He kept us all going in the same direction. He paid us very well for that time. He offered us many incentives as well. We made the playoffs about six times in a row after the Super Bowl. Not long after that Joe Gibbs built another great team. As far as the record books go, the Gibbs team may have been the best. They won three Super Bowls. And winning a Super Bowl is not easy to do, even less going back more than once.

11
Our Super Bowl Year

When we lost the 1971 playoff game against San Francisco, we were disappointed, but we knew we had a good team, and so did George. In the locker room after the game, he told us, "We made too many mistakes to win, but I know we'll have a championship football team next year." As 1972 started, the pressure wasn't really on us. Even though we'd made the play-offs the previous year, the entire 1972 season we still felt like we were just a bunch of old guys.

It was time for training camp, 1972. Training camp is the place where a team forges that sense of family. You're forced to be around your teammates day and night, on and off the field. You get everybody in the same place, where they are under control. It's basically like being locked up. They take you out of town. Training camp is a chance to build togetherness. You have new players coming in, fighting for your job. Whether you keep it or not is usually settled in training camp. Now, any football player's number one fear is losing his job. You're very, very lucky to be where you are. You play hurt because the minute you're out of the game, it gives your backup a chance to look good. You know that as soon as you aren't able to play the game at a very high level, that you will be replaced. That's the nature of the game.

The Redskins' training camp up was up in Carlisle, Pennsylvania, at Dickinson College. We stayed in the women's dorm. Carlisle was a small town, so it didn't take us long to find the local watering hole for a few beers after practice, though we made sure to get back by curfew, as George had bed checks.

Diron Talbert had a camper that he would bring to training camp, and the camper became a hangout. Anyone who wanted to get away and chill could go hang at the camper. It was off-campus, and sometimes we would go there and hang out and drink beer and take it easy.

Most people do not know this, but I walked out of camp one year. One preseason I was in negotiation for a new contract and it was not going my way. We were all hanging out at the local bar and I was disgruntled and decided that I was not going back to camp. Everyone left to make curfew and I stayed at the bar.

Then I started thinking that maybe this was not such a good idea. How could I get back to camp and into my room and not get caught?! No way I'm going to let George catch me. Then it came to me. I'll go sleep in the camper and then drive it back to camp at the crack of dawn and sneak in before breakfast. I called a cab and had it take me to the camper. I slept in it that night, then got up early in the morning. I unhooked the camper from the truck, and was going to drive the truck back to camp. As I drove down the road, people passing me and going the other way were honking and pointing at me. They did this all the way back to camp. I thought they were just doing that because they recognized me.

As I was sneaking in, I saw Diron going to breakfast. "Where have you been all night?" he asked. "Everyone is looking for you?" I said, "I stayed in the camper and drove back to camp." He asked, "Did you unhook the camper?" "Yeah," I said.

When we walked out to the truck, I found out I'd forgotten to unhook all the wires and the commode drain—in fact, I'd forgotten to disconnect everything but the hitch! All of these wires were ripped out and dragging behind the truck. The wires and the commode drain were destroyed.

Diron said, "You're going to pay to get this all fixed!" "Yeah, no problem!" I said. Come to think of it, I never did pay Diron back. I also didn't get my raise.

There was never a point in my eighteen-year career when I didn't worry about getting cut—even when the number of players on a team went from thirty-two or thirty-three to around fifty. In the old days, rosters were small. The rosters were so small that you didn't have a kicker or punter on the team who only kicked or punted. Punters and kickers used to be regular players. George Blanda punted and kicked and played quarterback. Running back Billy Cannon could punt. We used to have punting contests after practice to see who could punt the farthest.

In Buffalo, I did get a little more comfortable with job security. I knew the coach, and the Bills were very successful, winning back-to-back AFL Championships in 1964 and 1965. After I became a starter, I realized I might have a little advantage over another player trying to take my spot, but the bottom line is, no matter how many years you've played, everybody is trying to take your job. You knew that, and most coaches made you realize that.

But as I got older, it changed. With George Allen in Washington, he created a different atmosphere, with the Over-the-Hill Gang. I was playing with a bunch of guys in their thirties (the oldest, I think, was thirty-two), and I had a little more confidence knowing George brought us in because of our experience, and the team had a different feeling. I had the feeling that he'd let me play till I couldn't play, and that's how George treated us. He still brought in competition, and I knew that the end was going to come eventually. The end can come in many ways. It's a thing you live with and accept when you go into the league.

Training camp is crucial, not just for the rookies, but also for the older players fighting to keep their jobs, and it's taken very seriously. It was also important from a conditioning standpoint. Current NFL players would probably rather just show up and play and leave like a baseball team. It just doesn't work like that in football. Unlike today's NFL players, who basically train year-round, we would show up for training camp needing to get our bodies ready to play. We'd been off six, seven, eight months, because back in those days, you were working in the off-season. A football salary may have been nine thousand bucks, so you had to get a job in the off-season. Even when I went to Washington and got a fairly good salary, the job I worked in the off-season was necessary to make ends meet. Now, guys make a lot of money, and work out in the off-season at clubs or at the training facility.

Training camp also helped you prepare your body to reduce the risk of injury. After losing their job, the second biggest worry for most players is getting hurt. Back when I played, we did a lot of calisthenics. We ran in place and did jumping jacks and push-ups. We also did isometrics. You can fake isometrics. You would pick a partner and use their body as resistance. Buffalo, Jim Dunaway, and I did it, and we never worked too hard at it. I don't think they could tell. We had one guy in Washington who had us all lie down and do exercises on the ground. It didn't really look like we were doing anything. Allen didn't let us do that one in front of a crowd at a game.

The importance of weight training had also completely changed by the time I was a Redskin. At Nebraska, which now has a state-of-the-art weight room, our weight room consisted of a weight bench and a barbell. I rarely if ever lifted weights as a pro. One year, we got this new young kid. His official title was assistant defensive line coach, but he was hired as a weights coach for Redskins Park. He created weight lifting programs for every player on the team and posted these charts up on the walls above the lockers and we were supposed to keep track of our progress each day.

Well, I'd look up at these charts, and the new guys would have their charts all filled in, and some of the veterans would have something written down here or there. Mine was blank. I hate lifting weights.

Finally, the coach came to me and asked me why I hadn't been lifting weights. I told him it was because I was hurt. The coach went to the trainer and asked the trainer whether I was hurt. The trainer said, "If Ron says he's hurt, then you know he's really hurt."

Next the coach went to Torgy Torgeson and said, "I can't get

McDole to buy into the weight program." Torgy told him, "It's not my job to get involved in this situation. That's your job." "But McDole won't listen to me!" he said. Torgy said, "In that case, you're going to have to take it to George Allen."

George never dealt with anything immediately. He'd wait a while until he had the right time to discuss it. It was about a week later, and we were out on the practice field at Redskins Park. George would usually walk out on the field and wander around, looking at the trees, but instead he came up to me.

"It's amazing how well the season is going so far," said George. "We're 3 and 0. Why is that?" "Luck?" I said. "No," said George, "lack of injuries."

"Uh-oh," I thought. "I know where *this* is going. He's going to say that the weight program has cut our injuries." George remarks, as casually as he can, "So, I hear you're not lifting weights twice a week." (That was our minimum commitment.) I said, "I'm not." "Why not?" he asked. I said, "Okay, George. I never miss a game." "True, true." "And I'm never injured," I said. He said, "True again."

I stood back, held out my arms, and gestured at my physique. "George, it took me thirty-eight years to build this body, and I'm not letting some kid mess with it now!"

George looked at my pot belly and nodded. "It is rather nice." Finally, George sighed and said, "Don't worry about it." And that was the end of my close brush with the weight room.

We older guys liked to sit in the weight room and talk, but we rarely if ever used it to lift weights. One day, some of us older guys were sitting around in the weight room when a magazine photographer came in and wanted to take some photos of us using some of the new weight equipment. We were trying to pose, but we didn't even know how to use the equipment. When George Allen came by and asked what we were doing, and we told him we were posing for some magazine photos about the weight room, he kicked us out and got some young players for the photo shoot.

A lineman takes a lot of punishment during a game. In reality, you're supposed to be beating up the offensive lineman, not letting him beat you up. Still, you have instant contact on every play, and guards trying to trap you. That's tough because the guard is already working into a dead run. Everybody is plowing into each other, closing holes, grabbing the runner, and people pile on after the initial tackle. Thankfully, there's no leg whipping anymore, because it hurts like hell and you can break your leg. Your legs take a real beating on the line. You have pads, but once you hurt someplace, it's gonna stay sore, but during a game you don't notice. You don't feel pain because of the energy and excitement of the game, and the sound of the crowd. You're running on pure adrenaline. It's kinda like going to war, though I've never been to war. Wherever the ball went, I went. In Washington and Buffalo I always pursued the ball. That was my specialty. After the game, I'd be sore and dehydrated, but the human body is an amazing thing and in a few days, I'd be ready to go.

Another thing: I have never, in my entire career, taken a shot at somebody with the intention of hurting him. Some players do. Not many, but a few. In fact, when I was rushing a quarterback, and he had his back to me and didn't see me coming, I would yell loudly right before I hit him, so he would have a split-second to set himself.

Training continues all season long. During the season, a typical training week would be like this: After the game, you were ready to rest. If I hurt an ankle, I'd tape it up and walk on it all night to keep the blood out of the ankle. In Reston, we lived in a townhouse, and I'd walk up and down three flights of stairs, and by the next day, I'd be ready to go. We'd work harder Tuesday through Thursday. On Friday, we'd have a light workout, mostly short-yardage stuff. On Saturday, we'd stay at the Dulles Airport Marriott, and then play the home game the next day.

Before the season started, we had to get in condition and then play a series of exhibition games. These games are important. I realize it's a problem now with the longer season and the extended postseason, but that's just the way the game is played. The only guys who shouldn't play in preseason are the ones who are hurt.

The year 1972 was special. I'd been on the Bills when they won back-to-back AFL Championships, and 1972 was the year the Redskins went to the Super Bowl. The Redskins had not won a division title in twenty-seven years. I think that the best teams I ever played on were the 1964–65 Bills championships teams, but the year I had the most fun was 1972, the year the Redskins went to the Super Bowl.

Somewhere around this time, I got my nickname, "The Dancing Bear." Now, I know in part I got it because I do look like a bear, but there is more to the story than that. It all started at Paul Lucas's restaurant and bar, the Pall Mall, in Georgetown. Paul was a good friend of the team, about our age, and we'd hang out in there and have a good time. On one occasion, it must have been after a Monday night game, the television announcers Tom Brookshier and Pat Summerall were also at the Pall Mall, because they'd broadcast the game that week. We were drinking beer, and Sonny Jurgensen told me that he could dance on one of the bar's tables longer than I could. I jumped up there and Sonny and I started dancing. Everybody started laughing hysterically and saying I looked like a dancing bear. Sonny fell off the table first, and Sonny started calling me The Dancing Bear that night. Because Brookshier and Summerall were there, they picked it up and began using it on the air when they broadcast the game on television, so within a day or so the name was broadcast nationally. If those two hadn't been there, the name probably would have never taken off, but because of them, it stuck.

One time, not long after that, one of the Redskins' secretaries came in and said, "Ron, there are some senior citizens here that want to see you," and when I went out to visit them, they had brought me a huge stuffed bear. I still have it someplace. And later, I named my library furniture company Dancing Bear.

Before the 1972 season, George had a new helmet logo designed. Before Vince Lombardi had come to Washington, the

Redskins logo was a feathered spear. I must admit, I never paid much attention to logos, but I did like the one we got in 1972. Vince Lombardi had changed the logo from the spear to the letter "R," because he'd come from Green Bay and they have the big letter "G." When George took over, he changed the logo to the Indian. We started getting some of the newer helmets in 1971. If you look at photos of us playing the 49ers in the 1971 playoffs, we are still wearing the "R" helmets. Other than that first year in Washington, I played under the Indian head my whole career.

My first year we went to the playoffs. My second we went to the Super Bowl. The first year we were good. And the second year we were still playing well. The 1972 season started strong, with us winning eleven of our first twelve games. Billy played quarterback most of the season, ending the year tied for the lead in touchdown passes with 19. Larry Brown rushed for 1,216 yards, a 4.3 yard per carry average and was the NFL MVP and the AP Offensive Player of the Year. The Redskins defense had another solid year, with 5 blocked field goals, 4 blocked punts, and only 218 total points allowed—the lowest in the NFL that year. Our defense scored 4 touchdowns and made 17 interceptions for 287 yards. We also recovered 30 fumbles.

As the year progressed, the entire Washington DC area was swept up into Redskins mania. In a year filled with bad news at home and abroad, the Redskins were good news, and the city went all-out. Large crowds met us at the airport after away games. Autograph seekers showed up everywhere we went. Fans tracked us down; they told us what we were doing right and also what we were doing wrong. They wanted to talk sports with us. They talked to us like they knew us, because, in a way, they did. We were all over the *Washington Post* every day during football season. They cheered us on every Sunday, at the sold-out stadium, on television, on the radio, in the papers. They really did love us. And of course, we loved them right back.

One of my fellow linemen was Bill Brundige. Bill was the first player drafted by Redskins head coach Vince Lombardi in 1969.

A Colorado native, Brundige attended the University of Colorado, where he majored in physics. Brundige played seven seasons at defensive tackle for the Redskins, and remains sixth on the All-Time Redskins sack list. He was on the 1972 Super Bowl VII team, and blocked the field goal attempt by Dolphins kicker Garo Yapremian that led to a Mike Bass touchdown for the Redskins' only points in Super Bowl VII. He's also one of the 70 Greatest Redskins.

Now, Bill was a very good football player. He had a degree in physics, so he was also a highly intelligent football player. He knew what everyone was getting ready to do, sometimes even before they did. He picked up on everything in games—everything, everywhere, any position.

Bill would make our line calls and he had to know what to do in each situation. On the field, there is a pecking order, just like as the military. Our field general was our linebacker, Jack Pardee. Any order or play he called superseded any other play called by anyone else on the defense. If you heard your line caller call a play, and then you heard Pardee, you had to switch up instantly to the new play.

I loved when Bill was in. I let him call all the signals because he knew everything. He also knew whether someone was picking up our signals, and he would design our system to prevent that. If we were calling a stunt, we could try to hide it. Sometimes an offensive lineman was smart enough to figure it out from a nod, number, or other direction.

So, Bill used to make up codes, when he was in the game, so that we could change it up, if the other team was picking up our signals, like stunts. Bill would say something like, "If I give you a number over twenty, it means I'm rushing." Well, after a while we'd get the feeling that the offense had figured out our calls again. "I'll fix their ass," Brundige would say.

"I want you to take the first number I call, add it to the second number, and divide that by three. If the number is even, you go, and if it's odd, I go."

So, we would get up to the line. He'd call, "23, 15, 6," and then I'd be knocked flat on my ass. I would still be doing the math in my head when the play went down. That's when I would realize what it felt like to not understand what was going on the field, a problem some of our other linemen had regularly. I'd say, "Bill, I think we're getting a little too smart. Bring it down to my level."

Bill wasn't just smart, he was Mensa-smart, as in genius. We were sitting in a meeting one time, during a losing stretch. You see, if you lost two games in a row, it would be the end of the world. We were in the defense meeting, which was being run by George. George got up there and he was really upset. He was not usually the kind of guy who got upset about doing something wrong about the hole coverage. George was drawing on the blackboard about the holes. The linemen had numbered holes that we played in. George would get up and call on somebody: "Okay, Ron, how many yards did they gain in the 4-hole?" When he finished calling on me, he'd call on someone else, "What is the average in that hole?"

Brundige was sitting in the corner of the room BSing with Manny Sistrunk—"Yada, yada, yada." So George called on Brundige because he knew he was not paying a damned bit of attention to him. "Seven hundred eighty yards in this hole," he said to Brundige. "What is the average yards on this hole if they ran it five times?"

Brundige had the response in one second: "Sixty-eight yards." George asked him two more, and he did the same thing. Finally, George said, "Well, let's go on to something else." Bill could do math faster than a computer.

One time I was traveling with him, and before we boarded the plane he picked up three books at the airport. These were big, long books, not little books. By the time we got off the plane, he would throw them out because he had read them all on the plane. He was a speed reader and would turn the page like someone looking for a picture.

Bill recounted a few stories for this book about our experiences together: "I was going to sit down and write down some stories about Ron, but then I realized there ain't no way my fingers can fly across the keyboard fast enough to write everything down!

"Nineteen seventy was my rookie year. It was Vince Lombardi's first year as the coach in Washington, and Lombardi *owned* that town that year. I was the first player ever picked by Vince Lombardi in the draft after he became the Redskins' coach, so it was a big deal, and there was a big news conference. Then Lombardi died in August, and George Allen comes in. The first year, the Lombardi year, the Redskins had a terrible defense. And Lombardi told me, 'Bill, you're the bright spot on our defensive line.' Then, when George Allen replaced Lombardi, he made trades for Diron Talbert, Verlon Biggs, and Ron McDole.

"George valued veterans and experienced players. The first day of training camp, he told everybody, 'A rookie will never play for me!' Then, he got me aside and said, 'For your benefit, I'm going to treat you just like a rookie.' George told me, 'If you really work hard, you might start someday.' So, I went from being the toast of the town to being just another rookie.

"The first time I saw Ron McDole, I thought, 'So this big, fat, white guy from Buffalo is Ron McDole?!' This was at the first practice. I watched while he put on his jock strap and after he put it on you couldn't even see the jock strap because of his stomach. I started to think that maybe he wasn't as tough as they said. Then we went out to the practice field. We were running ropes and Ron ran those ropes so fast I couldn't even see his feet move!

"He had incredible balance. I played with him for seven years, and I never saw him knocked off his feet. He'd get hit and do a spin-move, and maybe lose a step or two, but he never got knocked down. He just had such great balance. He was so quick.

"I remember we were watching some game film from the previous year in 1971. The Redskins had played the Bills, so we were watching the film. The Bills had gone something like 2-12 in 1970, and I kept noticing that this left defensive end on the Bills kept making tackles 15 yards downfield on sweeps down the other side. This is a guy who is going all-out, hustling on every play, a guy who never gives up, on a team that is going nowhere, 2-12. That's just the kind of guy Ron was and is.

"Ron was a quiet leader. He reminds me so much of Kenny Houston. Kenny Houston never said a word, but he went out on the field and was such an amazing player that everybody respected him. That's how Ron was, too. George Allen liked to have a few players whom he would finger to be the spokesmen for George Allen in meetings. His two main guys were Diron Talbert and Brig Owens. Ron and Kenny didn't talk like that. I remember one time Kenny did talk, and everybody listened. But Kenny and Ron would go out on the field and play!

"The Redskins spent a lot of time in Georgetown, which is a very exclusive part of DC. Georgetown has great bars. Every Tuesday night was party night. All the bar owners in Georgetown knew us. The Redskins could walk into any bar and the drinks were on the house. Because the owners knew that if the Redskins showed up, the ladies and the fans would show up. The bars were always packed on Tuesday nights. Ron would roll in and raise his finger, and they would know he wanted a 'Silver Bullet,' which is a gin on the rocks. And my favorite song back then was the Beach Boys' 'Help Me Rhonda.' So McDole would get his Silver Bullet and we'd put 'Help Me Rhonda" on the jukebox and that was about as good as it gets.

"Washington was crazy for the Redskins. The Skins hadn't had a winning season in twenty-five years. We won our first five games and the town was going nuts! We went to Kansas City and played the Chiefs. That was the game where Charlie Taylor broke his leg. It was our first loss of the season. We were all really down in the dumps. As our plane got ready to land at Dulles Airport, back when there was nothing out by Dulles, you could see a stream of light on the Dulles Access Road. The road was backed up from Dulles Airport all the way to the Beltway. A radio DJ had suggested that the fans go out to meet our plane and welcome us back to town!

"In Washington in the early seventies, the Redskins were rock stars! The fans followed us everywhere. It was a magical time!

"Pat Fischer and Ron played together at the University of Nebraska, then briefly on the Cardinals, before ending up on the Redskins together. Those two were so much alike. Ron wore the old double-barred helmet facemask, and so did Fischer. They were both tough as nails. Before a game, Ron sat on a bench and chewed on a towel, and Pat would kind of nervously walk around in little circles.

"Ron was one of the best kick blockers the game has ever known. I remember he blocked one against the Jets but stung his shoulder and had to come to the bench. Verlon Biggs was standing out on the field, rubbing his hand as if he'd just blocked the kick. Ron wondered later why nobody had asked him about his blocked kick, and then he noticed people were talking to Verlon about it.

"'Verlon Biggs, you didn't block that kick!' he said to Verlon. 'Well,' said Verlon, 'you were over sitting on the bench, and someone had to take credit for it!'

"Our defensive front four may not have been the Purple People Eaters, and we may not have been the Fearsome Foursome, but we were a damn good line.

"George Allen assembled a team that had great chemistry. Ron, Diron, and I always knew what the other two were thinking. We knew what each other was going to do on a given play."

Bill's stories about those years also remind me of big Manny Sistrunk. Manny and Bill Brundige played next to me, and they would swing sometimes, which means they would switch in and out. They were the ones I communicated with all the time—I had to. One interesting thing about Manny was that he would be playing in the game and he would make these little noises. He was a tough ballplayer and he could hit and tackle people, that was for sure, but sometimes Manny would forget an audible. It was no big deal—we survived it. Bill and Manny were total opposites, but

143

they got the job done. If Bill or Manny was having a hard time, they could switch in and out. It worked and it was successful.

Any Redskins fan who attended or watched games from the sixties through the nineties will remember the gleaming, white, undulating exterior of Robert F. Kennedy Stadium in downtown Washington DC. It is the home of many Washington memories—the baseball Senators, the football Redskins, even the Beatles one night in August 1966.

RFK was built in 1960–61 as a replacement to Washington's former baseball and football stadium, Griffith Stadium. Opened in October, 1961 as District of Columbia Stadium, the stadium was renamed in January of 1969 to honor the slain U.S. senator and presidential candidate Robert F. Kennedy. RFK was one of the first so-called cookie-cutter stadiums, spherical in shape, intended for baseball and football. The Redskins played their first game in RFK on October 1, 1961, losing to the New York Giants 24-21. Their first win was over arch-rival Dallas on December 17, 1961. Appropriately, the Redskins' last win at RFK in December 1996 was also a defeat of the despised Cowboys.

Each conversion of RFK from football seating to baseball seating cost $40,000. This included a hydraulic pitcher's mound that could be lowered into the turf. The rolling bleachers allowed fans to jump up and down in unison and bounce the entire seating section!

Parking was sometimes a problem, as was the stadium's location in downtown Washington DC. Eventually, new Redskins owner Dan Snyder moved the team to a larger stadium in the suburbs. At its best, RFK seated only 55,000 fans, which meant less ticket revenue. The new stadium, FedEx Field, has seated as many as 91,000 fans, though its current capacity is advertised at 82,000.

We finished the season in first place in the NFC East, with a record of 11-3, right above the Dallas Cowboys. In the first round of the playoffs, on Christmas Eve, we played the Green Bay Packers at RFK Stadium, in front of our fans. The greatest games I played in were the playoff games. You either won or you went home, and you had a long time to think about losing. Green Bay played hard, and it was a tough, physical game. Knowing that the Packers loved to run the ball, we put five linemen on the line. Quarterback Bart Starr was forced into a passing game. The final score was 16–3. Billy Kilmer threw a touchdown pass to Roy Jefferson, Curt Knight added 4 field goals, and Larry Brown rushed for 101 yards. We were going to the NFC Championship Game.

On New Year's Eve, we faced our rival Dallas Cowboys. For the second week in a row, our defense did not let the opponent into the end zone. One of the greatest games, for me, was that first playoff against Dallas, the year when we went to the Super Bowl. People stepped up and played well. Everybody had been anticipating that it was the Cowboys who were going to go to the Super Bowl. Dallas managed only 1 field goal, Billy hit Charlie Taylor with 2 touchdown passes, and Curt Knight again booted 4 field goals as we won 26–3.

To me, the most fun time in football is when you are playing a game at the end of the season when you are going to the playoffs, and you are up by 20 points with two minutes left, and everybody is happy. It's a short period, because you must get ready for the next one, but that's the best feeling.

And the funnest games of the year, at least for Redskins and Cowboys fans, are the Redskins-Cowboys games. The rivalry is one of the most celebrated in professional sports. No matter what each team's season record is, all bets are off when the Redskins and the Cowboys face off. The duo has a combined 31 division titles and 8 Super Bowls. The rivalry has roots in Redskins owner George Preston Marshall first reneging on a tentative agreement to sell the team to Dallas businessman Clint Murchison Jr. followed by Marshall's initial refusal to agree to grant Dallas an NFL franchise in 1960. After this, Murchison bought the rights to the

Redskins fight song, "Hail to the Redskins!" from composer and Redskins band director Barnee Breeskin for $2,500. Then he held the song for ransom. If Marshall wanted his beloved song back, he had to approve the new team, and the Cowboys were in. In the expansion draft, the Cowboys took popular Redskins quarterback Eddie LaBaron. Coach George Allen took the vituperation to an entirely new level, and encouraged his team to do the same. A Redskins-Cowboys matchup is usually memorable. Who will forget Kenny Houston's goal-line stop on Cowboys running back Walt Garrison on October 8, 1973, or the Cowboys' 24–23 come-from-behind victory on Thanksgiving Day, 1974, when backup quarterback Clint Longley replaced an injured Roger Staubach with the Cowboys down 16–3 in the third quarter? The overall record as of 2016 shows the Cowboys leading the series 66-44-2.

When we got Kenny from the Houston Oilers, he was already an All-Pro, and the future Hall of Fame safety instantly became one of the main leaders on our team. Overall, Kenny played fourteen seasons, from 1967 to 1980, on the Oilers and the Skins. He had 49 interceptions with 898 return yards, 21 fumble recoveries, and 12 touchdowns. He was inducted into the Hall of Fame in 1986 and the *Sporting News* ranked him at No. 61 when naming the 100 Greatest Players of All Time in 1999.

He is an incredibly sharp, smart individual, and he is also the nicest, smartest, most professional guy I have ever seen on the field. But sometimes Kenny would go berserk! He'd get so mad he'd cold cock you with a forearm or something! What made this so unusual is that if you sat down and talked to this man for ten minutes, or thirty minutes, you would be impressed with how calm he was, and think he would never hurt a flea. I tell you what, he could punish you and he did it constantly. He was a big help when we needed him and a guy you wanted on your team.

As I was writing this book, Ken gave me some good stories. He told me, "When I first got traded to the Redskins from Houston, and showed up at camp, Ron McDole looked like an old man to me. I didn't understand at the time how good he was! I asked him once what his best move was. He said, 'I suck in my stomach and make my opponents miss me.'

"When I first came to the Skins, my roommate was tight end Alvin Reed. Ron would put on a baby diaper, just a big baby diaper, and then come knock on our door.

"Ron loved to play. He was tough. One game, he dislocated his elbow. On the way back from the game, on the airplane, he kept rotating the elbow over and over, and by working through the pain, he was able to play the next week. You never knew he was there. But he was always there on the field. He had a habit, before every game, of sitting in the locker room, quietly chewing on a towel.

"A lot of guys deserve to be in the Hall of Fame. It's unfortunate it's such a limited number. I was very fortunate to get in on the first ballot. Chris Hanburger retired before me, but he didn't get in till twenty years later. Ron deserves to be in the Hall of Fame. So does Pat Fischer.

"Ron's biggest strength as a player was consistency. You always knew you would get everything he had. And he played for such a long time. He retired at age thirty-nine. I retired at thirty-seven. That is a long life for a football player.

"Ron always had the same look on his face. You'd never know looking at him how funny he was, or how quick with a story. He was one of my favorite players and one of my favorite players to be around.

"Side note on 'The Tackle' against Walt Garrison in '73. That was the year I was traded to the Skins. I'd come from the AFC, and that tackle solidified me with the NFL. That was the most important play of my career."

After we played Dallas and beat them in the playoffs, we came into the meeting room that week and George told us we'd played so well that the team bought everyone a color television set! And there they were, all these big, boxed, color Sylvania television sets, stacked up, one for each player! Since Sylvania was in Batavia, New York, near my year-round home in Eden, I had mine delivered from the factory straight to the house, so I didn't to move it. The Over-the-Hill Gang was going to Super Bowl VII!

When we made it to the Super Bowl, the fans in Washington DC got *really* excited. Of course, we played our NFL Championship Game against Dallas, who was our arch-rival, and we beat them, so there was great anticipation that we were going to win the Super Bowl. I've always said—and people will agree with me—that our best game that year was the playoff game against the Cowboys. That game put us in the Super Bowl, and we deserved to go. But when we got there, we just did not get it done. The town went nuts that season. The whole city shut down so everybody could watch the Super Bowl on TV. So, when we lost, the fans were very unhappy. But they still congratulated us when we got back to town on the good year we'd had. As we came in to land at Dulles Airport, we could see a solid string of car lights on the Dulles Access Road, all the way to DC. It was our fans, coming out to welcome us home.

Once you make the Super Bowl you think there is no way to keep you from doing this again, and that if you just play the way you need to, that you'll get back. We were the Over-the-Hill Gang, and we had a lot of good, experienced guys who were in their thirties, and we had a good defense, so we thought we could get back there.

But when you get back on the road to get there again it is a long road and a hard road and lots of things have to go your way. People thought we could do it, and we did make the playoffs four or five years in a row. The fans were unbelievable in Washington DC. They were just as anxious to return as we were, and they kept track as to what was going on. It was just like Buffalo—you could not go into a store without someone chewing you out for having a bad game!

People need to realize that the Super Bowl we played in— Super Bowl VII—was one of the very early ones. It was not anything like the big mass production it is now. Basically, it was just another game. I guess you could compare it to a modern playoff game. However, it was THE THING to us. It was the end of the road, and every team wanted to win, and we did, too. But there wasn't the hype that you find with the modern Super Bowl. We had the press around a couple of times, and we had to be open to them, but it wasn't a media frenzy.

The thing I found to be the most difficult was trying to concentrate on the game, to a certain extent. We had so many people bothering us and then you have tickets to wrestle with, things like that. The team tried to keep us isolated at a motel, tried to keep the fans away so we could practice. George did a good job keeping us focused on what we were doing and why we were there—which was to win the game. We thought we would win the game, too, but we didn't. And as much as we tried to tell ourselves that there would be a next time, there wasn't.

The media hype was not as bad as it is today. There's no doubt about that. But we did have to make ourselves available the entire time we were out there. We had to be available for the press, and they'd take us to a field or stadium that had enough room for everyone and then we wandered around and answered all the reporters' questions. There were many reporters there; they came from everywhere, including your hometown, the city you played in, in fact pretty much everywhere in the country. I'd hate to see what it's like today!

Norv Evans was the Miami Dolphins' offensive lineman, whom I knew I'd be playing against. The reporters all asked me what I thought about him. I knew they had already been over talking to Norv so I asked, "What did he say about me?"

"He said you're good." "He's just as good," I said. I wasn't going to start anything. Mostly, though, it was boring, as we didn't have much to do except act a fool and like a bunch of kids. There are only so many questions a sports reporter can ask you. Finally, we'd get on the bus and go back to the hotel. Another thing that happened, though not to the extent it does now, is that many equipment companies would come and try to get you to wear their shoes, or their jackets, or things like that. They said they'd give us money for wearing the stuff. Not a lot of money. Then they would try to get us big linemen squeezed into their shoes that didn't fit. A few of us tried to wear them but it didn't work out, so we went back to our normal shoes. I do still have a pair of shoes I was given at the Super Bowl.

It was a great honor to play in Super Bowl VII. We anticipated winning it, but we still had to go out there and play the football game. We did not get trounced. We played like a solid defensive team, losing only 14-7 to undefeated Miami. There were situations during that game that could have won it for us, and there were things that happened, like the punting game. We were prepared. It's still hard to believe we lost that game. It was a good game, though maybe not high scoring. We were still in the game right to the last minute and I think we all thought we could win the game, but we just could not get it done.

Miami is still the only undefeated team to this day. That team deserved it. They played a long time and they were a very good team. I had a lot of friends on that team so I was happy for them. Our old Bills players Howard Kindig and Jim Dunaway got Super Bowl rings with the Dolphins that year. That 1972 Dolphins team might well be one of the best teams of all time, but I think we could have beaten them. The hardest defeat of my career was losing the Super Bowl.

The second-hardest defeat was in 1966 when the Bills lost that AFL Championship Game against Kansas City that enabled them to play in Super Bowl I.

You always think, when you play in a Super Bowl, you're going to get another chance to go back there, but let me tell you, it's not that easy. Few teams do it.

12

The Rest of the Redskins Years

I played on the Redskins for another seven years after our Super Bowl season in 1972. In 1973 we went 10-4 and made it to the playoffs again, where we lost to the Minnesota Vikings, 27-20. We repeated our record the following year. Our offense was ranked fourth in the NFL with 320 points scored, as was our defense, which held opponents to under 200 points. We had the old Ram Deacon Jones on our team that year, his last as an NFL player. One highlight was Deacon kicking an extra point.

In December, we went to the divisional playoffs, but were defeated by the Los Angeles Rams, 19–10, in Los Angeles. My roommate, Diron Talbert, was named to the Pro Bowl, as were Chris Hanburger, Kenny Houston, and Charley Taylor. I recovered a couple of fumbles but didn't get an interception.

Brig Owens was one of the stars of our defense in those days. He ended his career with 36 interceptions, and he's one of the 70 Greatest Redskins. Brig remembered some stories of our years together, and why those seventies Redskins teams were so unique:

"We had a sit-down strike one day at practice. George Allen had been working us really hard, and we decided to sit-down in protest. We all went out and did our stretches, and when George told us it was time to go, we just sat there.

"'What's going on?' asked George. Diron Talbert said, 'Hey, coach. We need a rest. We're working too hard! We took a vote and decided to strike.'

"George was thinking about that when McDole piped up: 'Hey, coach! It was all Talby's idea!' Just threw him under the bus!

"George Allen was a great coach. But the league didn't like him, the media didn't like him. That's because George went against all the rules. You know the saying 'the Redskins gave him an unlimited budget and he exceeded it,' and he traded draft picks he didn't have. And he stashed players that the league didn't even know he had. So, he got blackballed for years from getting into the Hall of Fame. When he finally got inducted, about thirty-five of his players showed up to support him.

"Another thing George did that was smart was that he picked up about nine or ten players who had been NFL Players Association union reps. A lot of these guys had been blackballed by other teams for being union leaders. These guys were all excellent players, as well. The league was into union-busting. But George picked up these union reps, because he knew that these were men who were supported by the other players on their teams, and that they were team leaders. He also knew that these guys would keep his team in line. As a result, the Redskins were a strong union team—maybe the strongest in the NFL. The Redskins were a hodgepodge of characters, but we were also a very disciplined team. We had a lot of fun playing together because we liked each other. We might not have been the most talented team but we didn't make a lot of mistakes. I know there were times when we went an entire week in practice without a mistake. George Allen hired officials to come to practice. He hired high school and college refs to come officiate our plays at practice to reduce mistakes and penalties. We were disciplined. And I also believe we were in better physical shape than our opponents."

Of Coach Allen, my teammate and cornerback Mike Bass says, "George Allen let us be who we were. I've never had a coach who showed so much respect to his players."

"As a member of the Redskins' defense," continues Mike, "we learned from George Allen the importance of working as a coordinated unit. This unit, defensive line, linebackers, and defensive backs, was dependent on each of us doing our part. When Coach Allen came to the Redskins, he saw that we needed some additions, particularly to the defensive line, and made the trades to make us real competitors.

Tommy McVean started out as the Redskins' assistant equipment manager in 1963, and became head equipment manager in 1969. He held the job for many years and knew all the Redskins players during his distinguished career. Of those seventies Redskins teams, he said, "Coach Allen and Chris Hanburger, our defensive general, knew more about the other team's offense than the opposing team's offense knew about itself. This was because, for one thing, the Redskins were a veteran team, and a smart team. It was also because Coach Allen had very long defensive practices, usually with meetings before and after practice. So, the defensive players were always ready. Playing the game was always fun for them because they were so well-prepared for it. It was an attitude of "let's get going!" They knew what they were going to do, and they knew what the opposing offense was going to do. And they knew what their teammates were each going to do. Our defense was always ranked in the Top 5 every year. We did this with a bunch of old guys who couldn't even run a five-flat forty.

In 1975 we slipped to 8-6 and a third-place finish in the NFC East. Sonny Jurgensen retired after a long and brilliant career. A personal highlight was the second touchdown of my career, on a fumble recovery. On September 28, against the New York Giants, I recovered a ball and took it a few yards into the end zone.

Probably the biggest play of my career happened on November 30, 1975. The season of 1975 was not one for someone with heart problems. We played three overtime games that season, and five that came down to the last play of the game.

That day, we were playing the Minnesota Vikings at RFK Stadium. The Vikings were on a roll, having gone undefeated in their first ten games. We were 6-4 and had to win our last four to make the playoffs. In the first half, we built up a huge lead, and in the second half, the Vikings got it all back again. Near the end of the game, the Vikings had taken the lead, 30–24. Billy Kilmer set up a touchdown throw to Frank Grant with long throws to Charlie Taylor and Grant. The score was 30–30.

All we had to do was get the extra point and we would win the game. When Mark Moseley put the ball through the goal post, we were up by a point with less than two minutes to play. Somehow, Vikings quarterback Fran Tarkenton marched his team down the field to set up Vikings kicker Fred Cox's 45-yard field goal attempt for the win. I switched places with Bill Brundige on the block attempt, and managed to get my right hand in there just enough to block the kick and let the Redskins win the game, 31–30. It isn't often that a defensive end wins a game. As a defensive end, you are expected to make sacks and tackles and so forth, but rarely do you get to do something that wins a game. That was a very fulfilling feeling for me. I tricked my blocker, Ron Yary, to block it. He knew I usually went inside and I took it outside. Ron later told me that I got him.

Billy Kilmer remembers this play, too. He told me about it for this book. Billy was and is one of the toughest guys you'll ever meet. He was a fearless, smart competitor who led us to the Super Bowl in 1972. We called him "Old Whiskey." In addition to playing in the Super Bowl, Billy also played in the 1972 Pro Bowl and was an All-Pro in 1972 and 1975. He led the NFL in touchdown passes and passer rating in 1972. Not bad for a backup to a Hall of Fame quarterback like Sonny Jurgensen!

As Billy relayed, "Ron, Pat Fischer, and I all came up to the NFL together the same year, 1961. Ron and Pat were drafted by St. Louis, and I was drafted by San Francisco. I remember playing against Ron in the college All-Star Game. The funniest story I remember of Ron was in one game against the Minnesota Vikings at RFK on November 30, 1975. The Vikings were 10-0 on the season at the time. After we scored a touchdown, Ron would always run up and shake my hand. We were playing

Minnesota, and their quarterback, Fran Tarkenton, was really giving our defense a bad day. They just could *not* stop him. In the last minute of the game, I ended up throwing a touchdown pass, which gave us a slim lead, 31–30. Ron ran right up to me after that touchdown pass, and instead of congratulating me, he says, 'You scored too early!' There were still 45 seconds left in the game. Sure enough, Tarkenton marches the Vikings down the field and gets them in field goal range with time almost expired, and the Vikings try a field goal on the last play in regulation. And who do you think blocks it but Ron McDole! That block won the game for us.

"Ron always had such a wonderful sense of humor. He had it at every practice, at every game, and every time we went out to dinner. You always got a smile when you were around Ron. Ron was one of the most gifted defensive ends I have ever seen. For his body type, he was so incredibly quick. When St. Louis Cardinals offensive lineman Dan Dierdorf got into the Hall of Fame, then I knew Ron McDole should get in, because in all those years playing against Ron, Dierdorf hasn't blocked him yet!"

In 1976, we picked up running backs Calvin Hill and John Riggins. Riggins would go on to become one of the key players in the Redskins' future. I picked up my third safety and had 2 more fumble recoveries. We won our last four games to end 10-4 and make it into the playoffs, but we lost to Minnesota, 35–20.

The 1977 season was also disappointing. We finished 9-5, out of the playoffs. Under George, we reached the playoffs five times, but couldn't get back to the Super Bowl. After we didn't make it to the playoffs in 1977 for the second time in three years, some people began to question George's philosophy. George was offered a contract, which he rejected, and he was let go.

Our old field general, Jack Pardee, had retired from playing and gone and had three successful seasons coaching the Chicago Bears. In 1978, Jack took over as Redskins coach. As a player, he'd run our defense for years. And Bobby Beathard came from Miami and became our general manager. Beathard's job was to rebuild the team, and he wasn't pleased when we won the first five games that year. He'd wanted to come in and take over a team that needed rebuilding. But then the Redskins fell apart. Jack was stuck between the Redskins' owner and Beathard. Beathard was the guy who selected players, and Jack wasn't playing Beathard's picks. Beathard sat in the box with the owner, it was either Jack Kent Cooke or Edward Bennett Williams, and second-guessed everything Pardee did down on the field.

Pardee released me in 1978, after the season was over. I saw it coming. My last year I'd gotten a pretty severe injury that affected my running, but I got well. But the injury meant I didn't play as much. It was the first time in my career that I hadn't played most of the time. The Redskins had a very good defensive end named Karl Lorch, and they were grooming him to replace me. There were little hints that my job was not safe. They used to say at training camp in the AFL that if your name is written on the back of your jersey in pen rather than sewn on that you needed to worry. I wasn't at that point, but another hint was when one of Pardee's line coaches told me I was not putting both hands down in the stance. That was something I'd never done in my career and I wasn't going to start now. And the thing was, nobody would have told me that before. Was I going to switch hands now, after eighteen years? Of course, I agreed, because I remembered Ed Henke's great advice: "Do what they tell you to do in practice. In the game, play the way you know how to play."

Near the end of my career, I did get to mentor some younger players who had great careers, guys like Dave Butz, George Starke, and Ted Fritsch. Part of football is the passing on of the knowledge of the game and the little tricks that let you have a long career. As Dave Butz recalled, "I was a real rookie on the Redskins back in the days of the 'Over-the-Hill Gang.' George Allen didn't like to use rookies because they made mistakes. I played as a rookie, but only after I learned a tremendous number of defensive audibles. One time we were playing the Miami Dolphins, possibly in the preseason. We were playing against Larry Csonka. The man had thirty-eight-inch thighs. With Csonka, you did not want to use your head to bring him down, but I had used my head in college and hit him head-on. I came out of that pile-up about a quarter-of-an-inch shorter. I overheard Csonka saying to Ron, 'When I run to the other side, not too much happens. But when I come to Ron's and your side, it seems like everybody hits me!' Between Bill Brundige, Diron Talbert, and Ron, I don't want all the money they spent on booze over the years. All I want is the *tip money*. It would be plenty. They taught me how to be a good tipper. I became like that after they retired. Ron McDole was a huge inspiration to me. It was an honor to play by him. He was always encouraging me. He was gracious, and he helped me a lot."

Another younger guy I liked a lot was George Starke. George ended up having a long career, all with the Skins. He played in three Super Bowls, including the victory in Super Bowl XVII. He was known as "The Head Hog" in the famous Hog lineup of Russ Grimm, Mark May, Joe Jacoby, and Jeff Bostic and was defensive captain his final five years on the team. He is one of the 70 Greatest Redskins. As George told me, "I played right tackle for thirteen years, and Ron played left defensive end, so when I think of Ron the first thing that comes to mind is that I had to practice against him every day.

"Games in the NFL are tough. You get beat up on Sunday, but you don't want to get beaten up during the week. On the Redskins, we had three tough practice days. The two toughest were Wednesday and Thursday, followed by Tuesday. We didn't want to beat each other up in practice, but the coaches didn't seem to understand this. They wanted full-speed, contact practices.

"When I started out, I was a kid and Ron was the veteran. Ron taught me how to pretend I was going full-speed against him without really going full-speed. In other words, we would create the illusion that we were going hard at each other when we were barely touching.

"It was carefully choreographed. If Ron was rushing me, his

coach Torgy Torgeson would be lined up right there behind him. It had to look realistic. We had it all planned, and we would take turns winning the drill.

"Later, after Ron retired, I was the veteran and we had a new kid named Charles Mann who was the rookie. I taught Charles Mann how to do the Ron McDole drill. We called it the 'Practice-Pretend-Contact-Dance-to-Keep-the-Coach-Happy Drill.'"

Another young guy I really liked was Ted Fritsch Jr. Ted remembers watching the Redskins as a rookie: "My rookie year, on the Atlanta Falcons, I took some friends to California to see the 1972 Super Bowl. Of course, we pulled for the old guys in the Over-the-Hill-Gang. So it was exciting when a few years later, in 1976, George Allen picked me up and I found myself on the Redskins, joining with the guys in the Over-the-Hill-Gang. I was a center, the deep snapper, and played almost exclusively on special teams. I backed up our starting center, Len Hauss, then after Len left, I backed up his replacement, Bob Kuziel. I was there through the 1979 season and was released before the start of the 1980 season.

"I was younger than the Over-the-Hill-Gang, and I didn't run with that crowd. Those older players were an elite group—Sonny, Billy, Talbert, Brundige, and Ron. They were so much fun to be around. Ron reminded me of my dad, Ted Fritsch Sr., who had played from 1942 to 1951 on the Green Bay Packers. Both looked like an everyday Santa Claus. They were both a little heavy, and both had a great sense of humor that left everyone in stitches.

"When I came to the Redskins, Ron had already played fifteen to sixteen years in the pros. I watched him to see how he performed. He was super quick, and very light on his feet. You could always count on Ron to make the big play. He had an uncanny ability, while he was engaged with a blocker, to be able to jump up and knock down passes. This ability really kept quarterbacks on their toes. If you looked at him, you wouldn't think he could jump, but he could, and quarterbacks had to deal with that. At the end of his career, Ron was still playing at a very high level. If you looked at him, your perception was of a big-bellied defensive end wearing an old two-bar mask. You'd think 'What?' But when you saw him on Sunday, he was a different guy! At game time, he took it to another level. He was blood and guts and balls to the wall on Sunday! On second and third down he was as tough as anybody. When our kicking team practiced, we always put Ron in the center of the attacking rush, because he had this tremendous swim move. When the Redskins let him go, it wasn't the same without him. He had a joy of life. He was and remains a real special guy.

"Ron had a business where he made school furniture in Winchester. He and his wife Paula invited my wife and me to come up and visit and see the operation. It was such a privilege for him to share that with me. He was proud of what he had done with his school furniture business. It was his way of giving back to the community. He and Paula didn't have to invite us. They did it to make us feel like part of the team. I was very touched by that.

"In the locker room, Ron could be a real comedian. He told lots of funny stories. George Allen had certain weights that each player had to weigh under their contracts. Weigh-ins were on Thursdays. On Tuesday, Wednesday, and Thursday, Ron dieted. But after weigh-in Thursday, nobody's lunch was safe on Thursday or Friday! Everybody brought an extra lunch for Ron!"

I was thirty-nine when I retired. Most football players are long gone by age thirty-nine. I'd managed to play the game for eighteen years, from 1961, in the second year of the AFL, through 1979. I'd been on two AFL Championship teams in the sixties. I'd also gotten the opportunity to go to the Super Bowl. I was offered a contract with the New York Giants for the next season, meaning I could have played to age forty, but I was done, and Paula said if I went to New York, I'd have to go alone. So, I retired. Since retirement, I've kept on working with my furniture business as well as going to alumni events for both the Bills and the Redskins. Buffalo has a great alumni program. They invite the old-timers back at the beginning of every season for a barbecue and tailgating session. A few years back, the Redskins picked their Top 80 players of all time, and I was honored to be picked.

Around 1979, I developed a relationship with the Timber Ridge School, in Winchester, Virginia, an accredited residential treatment facility for at-risk boys in grades seven through twelve. Timber Ridge started fielding a football team in 1974, and Vic Williams, who was coaching then, remembers that the majority of the boys had never played football; they'd only watched it on television. "The kids love the Redskins," Williams remembers. "Since Ron is a former pro, he makes an instant connection." As of 2017, I've supported Timber Ridge for thirty-nine years. Every year, there is a Thanksgiving banquet, and I present the Ron McDole Award to the student-athlete who shows the most character on and off the field. I also show up every summer for the annual Timber Ridge fundraising golf tournament. Sometimes I'll bring Pat Fischer along. Charlie Taylor and Mark Moseley have also attended. We auction off memorabilia signed by various Redskins.

Chris Taylor, who works at the school, told my coauthor that "we feel very fortunate that we made a connection with Ron. He understands the kids. Just by showing up, he shows them that they matter. He teaches them that if they get knocked down, get right back up again! These kids need to hear that. Many of them have been knocked down a lot."

If you play football at Timber Ridge, you play on Ron McDole Field. That makes me happy.

13

The Best of . . .

Many of Ron's fellow players point to his intelligence as being one of his greatest assets, along with quickness, consistency, and durability. What follows are Ron's observations on many diverse topics.

Reading the Offense

In eighteen years, I had a lot of opportunity to study running backs. I also had lots of opportunity to learn from other great players. The trick is to study each back's mannerisms until you can tell what he's planning to do. Pardee would watch their eyes. If there was a check-off and the back's eyes moved, you knew he was either going to get the ball or block. If his eyes didn't move, he wasn't in the play.

We also did something to draw the line in motion when they were doing a quick-count, meaning the line was going to take off from the first sound. Myron Pottios would call a quick-set. How did we know when that first sound in a quick count will happen? Because offensive players, linemen included, are creatures of habit. If the players come up to the line and they are not blocking, they tend to be more relaxed and take their time. On a quick-count, the player is tense. Then you know the play is going to that side.

As my career progressed, I got slower but I also got smarter. You can tell by the way the line moves up to the line whether there will be a quick-count. If the line walks up slowly, probably not. If the line rushes up, you can figure on a quick-count.

If a lineman is looking at you, he may be coming at you. If he's looking elsewhere, he's going elsewhere and the play is away from you. Players are creatures of habit. You just have to study and learn their habits and you can tell what they are going to do most of the time.

There are lots of little cheaty things that can blow out a big play, or blow out a first down. Guys line up differently for runs and passes, just little things that you learn to notice.

Quarterbacks also develop habits that help you read them. Joe Theismann developed a habit of lifting one of his feet before a snap. He did this over and over. Lenny Hauss, his center, tried to tell him he was doing it, but he didn't believe it. But in practice, we were ball-breaking him, beating the offensive line off the ball every time. Lenny finally said, "Okay, somebody is tipping off the defense." Nope, everybody said they weren't. It happened over and over. Joe's tipping was lifting his foot before the snap. Finally, Joe realized it and he fixed it.

The same way we would look for things to tip us off from opposing offensive lines, we would also look for things that our own offensive linemen were doing that might tip off another team and then tell them to correct it.

Down in the trenches, on the line, if you won 50 percent of the battles, you won.

The Best Players Ever

It's hard to say who the best overall player I've played with or against in eighteen years would be. To most people's minds, the greatest players would be quarterbacks. I didn't play against every quarterback, but the current players today, like Tom Brady, who sometimes call their own plays, are fantastic. Having a Brady is like having a coach on the field. Back in our days, Sonny Jurgensen was great. I didn't play that long with him, because he retired. Jack Kemp was a great quarterback and a great leader.

There are simply too many variables. There were so many guys who were great athletes. Plus, football is a team sport. You can be the greatest athlete in the world, but if you don't have anybody to block for you, you're not going anywhere. As with any sport, you don't just need the physical athleticism, you also need to have the mind to understand the game.

The greatest offensive lineman I ever went up against in the AFL was Ron Mix, who played right tackle on the San Diego Chargers. I was a left defensive end and he was a great pass-blocker and run-blocker, as well as one of the best overall players I ever faced. He was very hard to read, he was strong, and he was quick. In the NFL, Ron Yary was an outstanding tackle, very difficult to beat, very aggressive. Rayfield Wright of Dallas, who's in the Hall of Fame, was outstanding, but I had a lot of good games against him. He was an outstanding tackle.

It's also tough to pick a best quarterback. There have been so many, and I played in so many eras, that it's tough to pin down the best. One thing that makes a quarterback very hard to defend is having a quick release. I played in Houston with George Blanda, and later played against him. Blanda had a lightning-quick release. Blanda and Namath released the ball so quickly that it just made me angry. Even if the offensive lineman fell, you still didn't have time to get to him. Our job was to get the quarterback, and those two made it really hard. I didn't see Sonny Jurgensen play early in his career, because he was NFL and I was AFL, but when I was in Washington, he played very well. He was smart, a decision-maker. I also didn't like scramblers because they were so hard to get. Fran Tarkenton and I played on the same team, and came into the league the same year. When I played against him later, he'd drive me nuts. There are also a lot of forgotten players who deserve to be remembered. Earl Morrall helped two different teams get to the Super Bowl, and was a good, tough player, and yet he's kind of forgotten.

It's also difficult to pick the best receiver. I've seen so many great receivers over eighteen years. I played with some great ones, and I played against some great ones. I always liked the tight ends, because not only were they going across the field throwing blocks, but they also made catches. To me they were the best receivers. Then there were the speed guys, who could run fast and had great hands. One whom I played with was Albert Dubenion on the Bills. Another great one was the Bills' Glenn Bass. They helped us win the AFL Championship two years in a row. Charley Taylor in Washington was a great receiver, as was Roy Jefferson. Our tight end, Jerry Smith, was also a great receiver.

I think many players are underrated, or don't get the recognition that they deserve. I already mentioned Earl Morrall. He was good, but nobody gave him his due. But there are lots of guys who do their job very well every week and never get any press. They get lost in the shuffle. A lineman can block his man all game and nobody will know about it except for his teammates and the coaching staff. The press and broadcasters talk about underrated, but that's their job, not mine. Most guys play great games on the field and no one pays much attention.

14

The Dancing Bear Talks Football and Life

There are many questions that people may wonder about professional football, or the game as it was in the old AFL and the old NFL. I've tried to answer some of these in this chapter.

On showboating

One thing I can't stand is showboating. These players are ridiculous. They regularly cost their teams games. That never would have happened in the old days. Those players would have been gone the next day.

The hardest thing about being a football player and being a husband and father

One thing I always thought was kind of weird about being a professional football player is that you are in demand all the time. You are constantly giving your time to other peoples' kids and you do not do things for your own kids. For example, you are told you have to go to a certain place and give a speech, and you always have to try to pacify and keep everyone happy. And sadly, your own kids, and your wife, get ignored because they do not get your extra time. I have always felt guilty because I had to hurry here, go there, talk to some kids, go somewhere else, be somewhere else, and my kids are at home. But my own kids didn't expect me to come home because I didn't. It was very hard to figure out how to deploy your time. Most players who were fathers were terrible at it. So was I, because in my case my family came second.

On how his children saw him during his career—did they know their dad was a star player, and, if so, did they care?

I think the older they get they do realize I was a good player, but they don't realize all that it involved. When they were young, the team would have what we called "Kid's Week," where the players would pool our tickets (because we didn't get many) so that all the families could bring the kids to a game.

Normally, I would have to almost beat my kids to get them to go to the game. Going to a game just wasn't a big thing to them. After all, they see me every day, and they see all my friends, the other players, every day, so it wasn't a big deal. I almost had to drag them to go to the game, and because everyone else was bringing their kids and my kids didn't come, I would worry about that. With my kids, it was, "I can't go. I have to play soccer. I don't want to miss my soccer game," and I'd say, "It's only practice," and we'd fight about it. I wasn't the only player with this problem. We as players would kind of laugh about it. In the locker room, somebody would bring it up, "I have to beat my kids to get them to come to a game!" Still, it looks bad if you cannot get your own kids to come to the game.

It was very strange, because we as players were not really a big deal to our own kids. They would be playing soccer with kids who worshipped us, and they'd tell their friends, "Well, he's never home anyways." That kind of stuff.

A perfect example is this story from when I was on the Bills. We used to play basketball in the off-season. We would play against schoolteachers and such as a charity thing, and we loved to bring our own kids to watch. I took my daughter Tammy with me to a basketball game. The Bills had some very good basketball players. Ernie Warlick was good enough that he had a tryout with the Harlem Globetrotters. He was a big tall receiver on the team and a heck of a nice guy. Anyways, Ernie brought his kids, and I brought Tammy. I think I took her because nobody was at home to take care of her.

When it came time for us to sign autographs at halftime, everybody runs out onto the court and gathers around us. It was hard for me to keep track of Tammy. We go back into the locker room to get ready for the second half, and Ernie comes over to me.

"What's wrong with your daughter?" I asked, "What do you mean?" He said, "She's pulling on my shorts trying to get my autograph. I see her every other day."

Tammy didn't know Ernie was important until the charity basketball game. When she saw everybody else trying to get his autograph, she got a piece of paper from somebody and kept bugging him. And since she knew him, she thought he should immediately drop everything and sign it. It was a funny situation, but it happened, and that's the best way I can explain it.

On players and so-called free tickets to the games

Believe it or not, and I laugh when I say this, but it might surprise a lot of people to know that I never played with a team whose players got more than two tickets for the game. And the tickets were usually for the worst seats in the stadium both in Buffalo and Washington. Sometimes, we could *buy* up to four for *some* games, but again they were the worse seats in the stadium. When teams built bigger stadiums, I was still never able to buy more than four tickets, and they were usually for seats down low in the end zone. We as players had to pool our tickets to take our own kids, and if you had a lot of kids you had to get tickets from the other players and buy some of the tickets. That's basically the way it was for the teams I played with. Maybe it has changed now. I don't know. But I know everybody back then, and even today, thinks I can just go down to the ticket office tomorrow and get a ticket. Yes, I can, but I have to buy it just like everybody else does. And the same rules applied for away games basically.

How good was the equipment?

Most of my career we used an expansion helmet, with a strapping system, and your head sat in that and it kept your head away from the outer helmet shell. Later in my career they started bringing in what they called air helmets. They took the expansion straps out and put in air sections, one in the back, one on each side, on the top, and filled them with air. They were like plastic bags. There were three holes in the top and you had a little ball that you used to pump the sections up with air. They could hold a lot of pressure. Most guys pumped them way up.

I preferred to use my expansion helmet. Most guys did. We'd use the expansion helmet in practice. The only thing I remember that was a little funny with an air helmet was one time I hit somebody and the air bags blew out. The helmet was much bigger so the helmet dropped down over my eyes. After that happened, I think they put in a foam pad with air and pumped up the rest so that if it did blow out, you'd still have some form of protection.

Earlier in my career, I had seen guys with previous head injuries who put a foam pad on the outside of the helmet and molded it into the helmet's exterior. Billy Stacey on the Cardinals wore one like that after a head injury, way back in the early sixties.

Also, the larger face cages became very popular. Of course, I never wore the cage. I played eighteen years with a double-bar.

The equipment got better all the time. Today they have all different types of shoes. The shoulder pads got smaller. The mouth guard was added near the end of my career. I didn't like the mouth guard because it took up so much room in my mouth. As big as I was, I figured I needed as big an air intake as possible! Later a tooth guard replaced the mouth guard. Companies wanted pros to wear them because then all the little kids who played football would see them on TV and want to have one.

On the toughest games I ever played

I played 251 games, and they were all tough. There were certain teams that played very physically. Their style of play made it seem like they were trying to hit you harder, or come at you. The Chicago Bears are a perfect example. The Bears' tough defense really beat up our offensive people. Playing on the defensive line is tough. You know that some games are going to be extra physical. Most of the other AFL teams may have thought we played that way in Buffalo in 1964, 1965, and 1966, when we won the back-to-back AFL Championships and had a very physical defense and linemen.

As a defender, the thing I worried about most was the individual players, the great receiver or the great, physical running back. Those kinds of players could run on you and beat you up. They would just as soon run over the top of you as around you, and those were the kind of guys and teams you did not want to play. Of course, you didn't have any choice. The best thing to do was to get as ready for them as possible and to play physical and smart right back at them.

Grass versus artificial turf

We all hated artificial turf. Early in my career, no stadium had it. When I played in Houston, they had a natural dirt field. This was before the Astrodome. When AstroTurf first came on the scene, it was really a different feeling. Playing on turf is like playing on a basketball floor. You get a lot of mat burns. The turf can tear your uniform off. It was hard on your legs, like playing basketball on a basketball court. Your legs would get tired.

After they built the Astrodome in Houston, the Oilers had a special floor with a locker room where you went to borrow your special AstroTurf shoes. You had borrow shoes, kind of like what you do when you go bowling. There were two different kinds of shoes, lineman shoes and back shoes. We always wore the back shoes because we figured it would make us faster. The lineman shoe was extra heavy. I was always trying to use a lighter shoe, but most receivers didn't have size 15 feet.

Another thing about artificial turf was that when I got blood in my mouth, it felt very strange to spit on the AstroTurf. It was kind of like spitting on a carpet. And sometimes players have to throw up on the field. Other players also had this problem, so eventually teams put boxes next to the field for players to spit and throw up into.

George Allen had two fields made at Redskins Park out by Dulles, one of natural grass, the other of AstroTurf, though we only used the AstroTurf field the day before we had games on turf. If we were going to be playing on AstroTurf that week, we'd run a few plays on it, and that was it.

The funniest thing about it is that it looks like grass from the sideline and the stands, but it sure as hell doesn't feel like grass! And after the game you had to wash with a special soap or oil to prevent yourself from getting infected. And we'd tape our arms to keep them from getting hurt when we hit the turf.

On paychecks and medical benefits

When I retired in 1978, I was making a base salary of $110,000. It was a no-cut contract, plus incentives. We were classified in the same risk group actuarially as military or civilian test pilots, so premiums were completely out of sight for most players and we went without insurance. I was lucky, because I had a business and was insured. It was assumed that a professional football player's lifespan would be around sixty-five years because of all the physical contact and injuries, and I knew I would make it only a few years past that. I'm a freak. I managed to stay in remarkably good shape for eighteen seasons. I've never been a bodybuilder, and a lot of doctors are amazed that I've never had a serious injury. I attribute a lot of it to my distinct body type. I always say you can't pull fat like you can muscle, and you can't break fat like you do a bone! We had expensive insurance—so expensive that many retired players didn't bother getting it. We had no medical benefits. In fact, until Medicare, I didn't have good medical benefits.

The amounts of money were much less than a modern fan would expect. The years the Bills won the AFC Championships, we made an additional $4,000. In 1972, when the Skins went to Super Bowl VII, we each got $7,500 as the runners-up, and the Miami Dolphins got $15,000. And of course, you had to pay taxes on this, and that wiped out a good portion of it.

On modern players

There were no agents back then. We did all kinds of things for free for the community, visiting hospitals and signing autographs. These days, guys won't do anything for free, because their agents don't want them to. It's all about money.

Players play more games per season than we did. Fourteen games are plenty. Back when we had fourteen games, you really had the potential to play seventeen. We played seventeen the year we went to Super Bowl VII. Sixteen is a long regular season. Players are bigger and better trained nowadays. This helps them make it through the season. We never trained to be football players. When I was in school, I played football for the education and not because I was trying to make it in the pros. Now you have fathers training their kids to be professional football players from age five. And the money is so much different now. We made $9,000 a year. Now players make $9 million. When I was young, everybody considered pro football players to be big and dumb. I didn't meet many dumb football players. You have to be very intelligent to play pro football. If you're not, there's always somebody waiting to take your job.

Some modern athletes have good attitudes. I was very impressed by Robert Griffin Jr. when he played for the Redskins. He came to town and the first thing he did was find out who his linemen were and called them up. Most modern athletes do not. They don't give a shit that their high salaries come from our hard work building the game into an American institution. But it's not just because of the league: it's the different way people are brought up these days.

On the platoon system and endless player substitutions

In college, you played both defense and offense. You never came off the field. Back at Nebraska, I think I logged the most time— 4,000 and some minutes over my college career. Going into the pros at that time, they played a two-platoon system. In college, you might have been a great player both ways, but when you went to the pros, they had to decide on which way to play you, which way you fit best. A lot of guys who were good in college didn't make the pros, because although they were good on both offense and defense, you had to be outstanding one way or the other. There were a few players, like Chuck McNair on the Eagles, who did still play both ways. He played center and I believe he also played linebacker. Another thing about the pros is that if you weren't a starter, you really needed to know how to play all the positions. If you were an offensive lineman, you had to know how to play all the positions. On defense, you had to know all the defensive end and tackle plays.

How did old-school players manage to stay in and play the whole game?

Conditioning and excitement. Excitement, especially when you're at home and you have the crowd behind you. When you get in there, time is nothing to you. You hurry up all the time, reading the formations, getting up to the line, and there isn't a lot of time. I always went on the assumption that if I were hurt to the point to where I could not help our team, I wouldn't be out there; otherwise, I'd get taped up, or fixed up, and play.

Old-school players liked staying on the field the whole game. In fact, it used to be a rule that if you went off the field, you couldn't come back in until the next quarter. I really don't like the modern platooning of players, where players only play for specific plays or downs.

The only time I came off the field was when George Allen put Jimmie Jones in periodically for a play or two. George's reasoning was that on passing downs, Jimmy was smaller and quicker. George thought that the change of pace could make a big play for us. You never like to come out of the game, but by switching players up, you can create a better situation. You want to match your stronger player against their weaker player. The platoon system is just a highly developed form of that.

George Allen always said, "If you want to teach people how to play football, then go coach high school or college. That's where they're supposed to be taught. I don't have time." And he never did.

On medical care

Depends on the doctor. In my early days, the doctors were usually guys who were big fans, but gradually medical care got better and better. As the league got more successful, everything got better. In the old days, somebody would just look at your eyeballs and ask how many fingers he was holding up. Now teams have advanced care and surgeons and the whole bit. But even when I was playing in Houston, and having all the problems with my migraines, the Oilers doctor, Dr. Rivers, was excellent. He lined up specialists for me. Surgery has changed radically, too. We didn't used to have arthroscopic surgery. They had to cut you open to fix you. They'd cut you up and put you in a full cast and you'd be done for the year. Now, it's less invasive.

Buying insurance was atrocious. You couldn't buy insurance because medical insurance was so expensive. We do have the 1988 plan that supplied around $120,000 a year for players who are in a home, or in assisted living, but there are only 20–40 players currently using it.

Concussions

I'm not sure whether I ever left a game from a concussion. Yes, I did. I hit my head on Larry Csonka's knee on the goal line one time and had to leave.

Because of my experiences early in my career with migraine seizures, which basically almost cost me my career, I was very nervous when I was hit in the head, that they would take me out of the game, and I'd end up in the hospital, and I might never get back on the field again. So, I just sucked it up. I was very fortunate that I never suffered a serious head injury, or a serious injury of any kind.

How were concussions diagnosed and treated?

You'd see some guy out laying on the field, or staggering around, and it was obvious he'd taken a hard hit to the head. The trainers would take the player to the sideline and do some basic tests, like holding up fingers, or asking some questions. We always joked that if the guy being questioned was our starting quarterback, and he was being asked how many fingers, we other players would stand behind the doctor and flash him the answers because we didn't want him to leave the game! Concussions are taken much more seriously today. Now, if you get a concussion, there's protocol and you are automatically removed.

How well have former players been taken care of when they experience brain trauma years later?

It seems to me that, even though we were talking about a head injury—an injury involving your brain—that a head injury was not seen the same was as a knee injury, which could keep you out of a game. If you felt better the next week you could play. The main thing they did was keep players out of games to rest. I know it's kind of dumb to say this, but it just wasn't a big deal. Years later, head injury is being taken much more seriously.

It's funny. There are two things all fans assume about professional football players. One is that you get tickets to the games. The other is that you get taken care of after you retire. No. When you're finished, you're finished. The league doesn't send somebody around to check on you. At one point, we couldn't even get the medical records of our own injuries!

Pat Fischer's cognitive issues and link to head injuries

About eight years ago, Pat started getting a little memory loss, which happens when your body begins to age. Nothing bad. Just simple things that I now experience myself. His memory loss just started earlier. But it got worse over time. Pat lived that way by himself for a long time, with nobody to watch him. Two to three years ago, he got examined, and since then it's seemed to have stayed at the same level. He doesn't drive anymore. He knows how to get somewhere but he might not know how to get back. He's in a program now and doing great. You wouldn't know anything was wrong with him unless you knew him. I've known him for fifty years, and I know him well and he knows me, and most of the time, he seems the same.

As to the former players with brain issues, I know of four or five, and they really aren't getting treatment. I can assure you that when Pat and I started playing, we never had one thought about having a concussion or being injured. We understood we could get banged around. But we did not know how serious it could be. We didn't know because nobody told us about the dangers of head injuries. Kind of like smoking cigarettes. My father died from smoking cigarettes, but he didn't know they could kill you because at that time they didn't announce the fact that smoking would kill you. If he'd have known, I assure you he would have quit.

On keeping in touch with old teammates

After your career ends, you don't see your old teammates much anymore. I still see the Washington players who continue to live in this area, but I hardly have any contact with former Bills teammates. As an alumnus, a former player, you are usually forgotten. Football, and life in general, is all about what you can do *now*, not what you did. It's a shame. You don't usually know when a former player dies. It's something we're all trying to get used to, as we get older, the way you lose contact after your career with people you shared so much with.

Roommates

In my eighteen years in the pros I had only three roommates. In Buffalo, I had two different roommates, George Flint and Jim Dunaway. On the Redskins, I had only one roommate, Diron Talbert.

Jim (Dunaway) was a big country boy from Mississippi, a real smart, real tough player. One year he came into Buffalo early to get a place to live for the season, and the family came up. He called me and said, "I need your help."

"What do you mean?" I asked tentatively. He said, "I'm trying to rent an apartment here in Buffalo." "Sure, I'll help you," I said. "Come on up to the house."

He showed up shortly after that, and I asked him where the apartment was that he wanted to rent. He said it was in the Lakeshore area.

"Okay," I said. "What's the phone number? And why do you need me to call instead of you?" He said, "I did call. I called them twice." "So, what's the problem?" I asked. He said, "They think I'm black. When I talk on the phone with my southern accent, they think I'm black and they tell me there's no room available. Then I called back half an hour later and they said the room is still not available. So, if you call them, Ron, they won't know it's me."

I thought he was just BSing me, so I called and said, "I'm interested in renting that apartment you have down in Lakeshore." They said, "Oh, no problem. Come down and see it anytime."

We drove to the apartment and here is this big white guy who makes me look like Mary Poppins. I don't think he knew I'd called. Jim and I were both white. I didn't make a scene or anything.

Jim and I were not allowed to eat at half the smorgasbords anywhere in the cities where we played football—a smorgasbord meaning a place that lets you eat all you can eat. One year, the Bills team played an All-Star Game in Houston against the AFL All-Stars. The AFL team that won the championship had to play the All-Star Game. I was late getting down there to Houston because one of my kids was being born—I think it was Mick. I had to fly down to Houston separately and I guess there was sort of flu going around down there in the hotel we were staying at. At the top of the hotel they had one of those all-you-can-eat kind of restaurants, the kind where they will feed you by the shovelful.

I flew into town and Jim picked me up at the airport in a car he'd borrowed from someone. He looked terrible. I asked him what was going on.

"Everyone on the team is as sick as hell," he groaned. "There's some sort of flu going around." I said, "Oh shit, now I'll probably get the flu." Jim said, "Oh no, I got a plan. We are going to out-eat the flu!" I asked, "Out-eat the flu?"

"Oh, yeah. I got it all set up. We're going up to the hotel restaurant in about an hour and we are going to eat all we *can* eat and we will out-eat the flu!"

I got checked in and we went up the elevator. We got to the restaurant and we could see that they knew these two big guys were going to do some serious eating! We started eating and eating and eating, and drinking milk. Jim could drink two pitchers of milk in five minutes. We were eating and eating, and they were bringing us more food, and we kept eating. It wasn't very late yet, maybe four in the afternoon. And I swear that we out-ate the flu, because the next day we felt like a million dollars. And it was a treat, because every buffet restaurant in Buffalo had banned us. They told us we ate too much.

In Washington, my roommate was Diron Talbert. He was a Texan, but he hated the Dallas Cowboys. He loved playing Dallas and stirring up feeling before the game. He once chased a neighbor kid who'd come over to our house in Reston. This kid came over wearing Dallas Cowboys pajamas and telling Diron and me that the Cowboys were going to beat the Redskins that week. Diron chased that kid around the house and threw him out the door.

I could tell stories about Diron forever. We ran together. What a great guy—a rowdy kind of guy. The kind of guy who gets thrown out of a bar. He lived in Texas and was an old Texas boy. But he hated the Dallas Cowboys. He liked to drive the Dallas Cowboys crazy, not only on the field but in the newspapers. I think George Allen was paying him to write some of those articles! Poor Roger Staubach, I think he took it personally every time Diron said something about him, which was *often*!

Diron was a great football player; he played on the right side. He was an excellent leader who knew how to get the job done. If he disagreed with something, he would tell you. Sometimes, he would get in a little trouble with his mouth. If you wanted something done from George Allen, he was the guy to talk to. He knew George pretty well because he'd played one or two years with George on the Rams before George had brought him to Washington. Diron was like George's illegitimate son; he could talk to George about anything. He was a big promoter for George when the Over-the-Hill Gang was forming. Guys would come to the Redskins—which was a team that generally got beat up, but had some good players like Chris Hanburger, Larry Brown, and Lenny Hauss—and he would be the one who could challenge George. If you needed to get to George, you went to Diron. He also got everyone together to follow George.

He was always promoting something, a natural salesman. And he loved to play practical jokes. He was loud and fun.

Diron almost never got hurt. He was in the middle of everything, and he led on the field. If one of the linemen dropped it down, he would be all over you and nine times out of ten he was right. You need someone like that around most of the time and he was the one. We hung out together most of the time. He was a very nice person, no doubt about it, but a little rough around the edges when he got going. That was just Diron. And you had to love him. I asked my old roommate for some observations for my tome, and he has the following tales.

Diron Talbert remembers: "I roomed with Ron six or seven years on the Redskins, and we hung around together a lot during those years. I'd played on the Los Angeles Rams for George Allen, and he brought me and a bunch of other Rams to the Redskins when he became the head coach. Up at training camp, at Carlisle, Pennsylvania, we were always looking for things to do in our free time. We practically lived at the bar. And Ron always liked Carlisle, because while we were at camp, a circus came to town. All the players would go and watch the fucking circus. Then the players would put on their own circus, and Ron would get into all that shit. We lived at the bar in our off-hours at training camp. There were a lot of us old Rams and we hooked up with McDole, Pat Fischer, and Billy Kilmer, and Ron was the ringleader.

"We used to go to a club in Georgetown, on M Street, called the Pall Mall Club. It was owned by a friend of ours named Paul Lucas. We'd park our cars across the street, and go in. Ron would go up to the bar and order a glass of gin with ice. They'd bring it out and the next thing you know he'd be gone! He'd be out on the dance floor! He'd start dancing, and he'd dance for one or two hours straight, and his gin would just sit on the bar with its ice melting. This was the disco era. He'd sweat all the way through his shirt and t-shirt, and he'd be grabbing bar napkins to towel himself down.

"The thing that made Ron such a good player was that he was so consistent. He had a lot of great moments, but he had many, many good moments. His good moments are what kept him in the league. He was consistently good. He rarely made a mistake. We would watch game film every week, for one or two hours, and analyze our play. So I know. I also don't recall him ever getting hurt.

"Before each ball game, he would know exactly what he wanted to do. He had studied the person across from him (on the offensive line), and put together a game plan. And then, if needed, he'd be able to alter it. Ron knew how he was going to play the game before the game even started.

"I think by the time he roomed with me, Ron had mellowed out with age. He quit doing a lot of the silly shit that players do. But he was silly on the dance floor, that son of a bitch!"

Are NFL players disposable and being used by the owners to make money?

Yes! I mean, think about it. We play a game, a sports game. You have baseball, basketball, all kinds of team sports. It all started with a bunch of guys who got together and started to play. And they got better and better to the point that other people would pay to watch them. And owners are always trying to find somebody good to put out on the field and make them lots of money. It's all about money.

When the players are in need, will owners help them?

I don't think that is always the case. Players are hired to do a job. When they can't do it, they're cut loose. Most owners are pretty good if you are playing for them, and playing well. They treat you well because they want you to play well for them. But in the old days, if you wanted to play for a different team, you couldn't switch. The owners would take care of each other. Players are always trying to get more money, and owners are always trying to keep salaries down.

In the sixties, you'd be shocked to find out a guy who came to your team and was a star player might make $15,000 a year and somebody would join the team with about the same ability and he'd make $100,000 a year. Some teams were better than others. The Rooney family in Pittsburg was always good to its players.

Best team of all time

Obviously, I guess that would be Miami, whom we played in the Super Bowl. They made it through an entire season undefeated. But it's hard to say. So much has changed since the early sixties. Plus, there used to be two leagues. We'll never know whether our 1964–65 Buffalo Bills team was as good as the NFL teams of the era, because we only played AFL teams. But we may have been the best team. We certainly were one of the best teams in the AFL in the sixties. Another great team was the Baltimore

Colts. The Patriots are an amazing team, or have been. But on any given day, any great team can get beat.

Strangest weather you ever played in?

Well, I spent eight years in Buffalo, and you know what's going to happen up there! We played in some unbelievable snowstorms there! In Washington, the weather was better, but the year after we went to the Super Bowl, we played a playoff game up in Minnesota and it was 28 degrees below zero. And we had a similar game up there the very next year. It was about 25 below zero. We lost both games. But that wasn't the reason. Both teams played the weather. I know when I went on the road when I was in Buffalo, we'd have to travel west and play Oakland one week, then stick around and play San Diego the next week, so we'd have to practice in the heat, which would kill us, because we were used to playing and practicing in 30 degrees in Buffalo.

You were a regular guy who didn't make millions. Do you wish you played now rather than then?

That's an easy question. Yes! We didn't make a lot of money. I signed for $9,250, as a third or fourth draft choice of the Cardinals. And my captain at Nebraska, Pat Fischer, was also drafted by the Cardinals. We both felt surprised that we were being given the opportunity to play professional football. I recall sitting with Pat in the student union after our last college season was over and we both had to go back to school. I had to go back and do my student teaching and get my degree in education, and Pat needed some classes for whatever he ended up getting. He kept changing his major. Anyway, we talked about how we'd both been signed and given the opportunity to play professional football. At least we could say we tried. Pat was very small for the National Football League, or any league, but he went on to play seventeen seasons, and he certainly deserves to be in the Hall of Fame for the career he had.

The money didn't really get big until we left the game. And sometimes I wonder what it would have been like to have played later. But, hey, I wouldn't pass up my experiences playing in the National Football League, playing all those years, not really getting hurt, and the people I associated with, and played with. It's been interesting to see what professional football has grown to today. I always knew it would be good after the AFL and the NFL joined together. Now it goes on all year long. Teams have their own year-round shows, their own stations, even their own criminal element. Even though the game has changed drastically in many ways, you still have to block and tackle and knock people down and that's what makes it fun. I hope the league doesn't get destroyed with the possibility of all the concussions. The future? No one knows.

Was football a better sport then or now as far as fan excitement, strategy, and so on?

Football was exciting from the beginning. Though my first love was baseball, even in high school, I'd been in awe of the big college sports rivalries. Being from Ohio, it was all about Ohio State and Michigan and the rivalries were unbelievable. And Nebraska was the same way. People would pack the stadium from all over that part of the state. The fans and the excitement have always been there in football. Especially on the college level. I played nine years in the AFL and nine years in the NFL. Every year football got bigger and bigger. And nobody had any idea how big the Super Bowl would become. By the end of my career, I'd be down there on the field and look up in the stands and I couldn't believe how many people were watching.

In the early days of the AFL, it wouldn't be much different on the field from a high school or college game. AFL attendance wasn't great. Now, in Buffalo, it was great. But when I played for the Houston Oilers, we were like the fourth game of the week on a high school football field, Jefferson Field I believe it was called.

Afterword

Reflections from My Family

Paula's Story

What was it like to be a professional football wife? It depended on the day, and hindsight is 20/20, but all I really think of is the laughter. There was a small percentage of married players, and we were all in the same boat. Players didn't make a lot of money. How many women were looking to marry a football player making $9,500 a year? Ron could have made about $4,500 teaching school. We were both twenty-one when we got married.

I went to Purdue as a competitive diver, then transferred to Ohio University, and finally to the University of Nebraska, where I needed one class to graduate. I'd taken all pre-med courses at Purdue.

At Nebraska, there were maybe eight married couples on the team. All had babies. We'd put up the wooden gates, put the toys in one room, and go and play bridge and mahjong all afternoon.

We lived on Wren Lane in St. Louis. It was a housing subdivision where every house and every street looked the same, a subdivision of apartments and duplexes. You could easily turn down the wrong street and never know it.

In Houston, I personally hated it. We stayed in a motel. George Blanda and his wife were right downstairs. Taz got pneumonia from the humidity and we couldn't get him straightened out. Ron got his migraines and he got cut and went back to Nebraska after five games. I never made it to Minnesota; it was just too short a time Ron was there. The Buffalo Halloween parties were such a hoot.

In Washington DC, Sharon Mosely and I started a wives' football lecture series at Woodward & Lothrup, designed to help wives understand football. This was after I got a temporary job at Woodward & Lothrup one Christmas that I ended up keeping for two years. I took advantage of my employee discount to get clothes for myself and the kids during that time. (Ron says I spent more than I made). We taught the wives how to understand football. We started with a group of about ten wives and ended up with about twenty-five. It was a real teaching session, with *X*'s and *O*'s, and it got written up in the *Washington Post*. From then on, the *Post* did regular articles on the Redskins' wives and kids. Those were fun times, but I was probably most happy at home, taking care of the kids.

Tammy's Story

My earliest memories are from Buffalo. Even then I got the family atmosphere between the players and families. They were all about the same age and all in the same boat—not making any money, trying to raise a young family and make the new American Football League work.

As a little girl, I knew my dad played football, but he also built houses. I didn't think anything of it. Playing football was just what my daddy did—no big deal. I never went to any games; I was too busy playing outside.

When I got old enough to start school, I started getting asked by other kids for autographs from my dad. I thought it was silly but I would ask dad and he would always sign. Around first or second grade I figured out that I could make money by selling Dad's autographs at school. I would charge five cents for an autograph. This turned out to be a limited business because there weren't many people in Eden. However, my mom found out and I had to give all the money back.

The Bills were always doing something for the community. I remember one time Dad took my brother Taz and me to a local high school for a charity basketball game. Dad was not the best basketball player. During the game, Dad lay down at center court, put the basketball on his belly, and then Paul Maguire, the Bills' kicker, grabbed one of Dad's legs and pumped his leg like it was a car jack. Dad's belly puffed up with each pump until it was at the right height, and then Paul kicked the basketball like a field goal, and it went into the basket! The crowd went crazy!

I remember the day my dad got traded. I had been out playing down the hill and got called in for dinner. Mom was running around getting Dad all dressed up. I asked what was going on. Mom said, "Your dad got traded to the Washington Redskins." I had no idea what that meant. During that whole trade process, that is the first time I remember seeing my dad on TV, which I thought was cool. He was on the news with Paul Maguire and they were talking about the changes with the Bills.

I was older now and understood basically what Dad did. I also found out that people wanted to know me and hang out because of Dad. You learned early who wanted to be your friend because of you or who you knew. I was lucky, because I played sports, so I made a lot of friends and played lots of sports. There was always a pickup game of something going on in the neighborhood.

When it was June in New York, Dad would start "training" for training camp. He played lots of racquetball and handball. I remember he would load us kids in the station wagon with him to the high school track. He'd have a full rubber suit on, and he would run laps, sprint, and do push-ups and sit-ups. We'd sit on him while he did push-ups, or sit on his feet and hold his legs as he tried to run. Then we would hit Dairy Queen on the way home.

I also remember that Dad really could not play with us. He could not afford to get hurt. But sometimes we would wrestle. Sometimes he'd hit baseballs so we could catch them, but he hit them so far out into the field that we spent hours looking for them. He had some favorite sayings when we were growing up.

If I asked him where he was going, he would answer, "Crazy. Want to come?" Sometimes he would tell us, "Don't touch me, I'm a star!"

In the middle of July, Dad would leave for training camp. Mom would pack us up and we'd move the beginning of August to Reston, Virginia, when Dad was on the Redskins. When we got there, training camp would be almost over. We'd start school and go until Christmas break. We then moved back to New York for before New Year's. I did that from fifth through tenth grade.

A funny story about when I realized why it was so hard for Dad to come to my games. I was playing on a flag football team up on Hook Road in Reston. One of the rules of the game is that no one can stand on the sideline from the 10-yard line to the end zone. Diron Talbert had come over to visit Dad, and they decided to come watch. He and Dad walked up the street and stood near the end zone on the side away from everyone. They were instantly mobbed for autographs and our team got a 10-yard penalty. I went over and said, "Thank you guys for coming. Now, could you leave because you're costing us yards!"

I babysat the other Redskins players' kids on Sunday. I would go to Moseley's house, and sometimes it was other kids too. I would spend the night there and Mark would drop me off at school in Herndon on Monday morning because he had an early radio show. I could watch the game on TV and get paid for it. I was one of the oldest Redskins players' kids in Washington. Billy Kilmer had a daughter who was older, but she did not live with him. So, I was the Redskins' resident babysitter as needed.

Mom went to all the home games in Washington, and there was a group of wives who would go to the games, and they all sat together on the 50-yard line. We went to only one game a year, typically the last home game of the season, because Coach Allen would have an end-of-season party for the coaches and players and their families. We always sat in the free seats in the end zone near the band while the wives and girlfriends were on the 50-yard line and met Mom in the tunnel after the game.

There are two games I specifically remember. One was the Minnesota game. We were going because we were supposed to meet Mick Tingelhoff (my godfather). It was a tough game, because Redskins fans are fickle. They were either hooting and hollering or cussing and screaming, "We want Billy!" or "We want Sonny!" No one sitting around us knew who we were, but I was mad that they were booing any player. We were winning by 1 point and time was running out. The Vikings marched down the field, and with basically no time on the clock they were going to kick a field goal that would have them win by 2. Dad blocked the field goal and the Redskins won! By the time we got down to the tunnel I missed seeing Mick because the Vikings were so pissed that they did not even change. They just walked off the field, got on the bus, and left.

As far as players, there were not many I did not like. In Buffalo, I loved Paul Maguire, Tom Sestak, Ernie Warlick, Jack Kemp, Al Bemiller, Joe O'Donnell, and Jim Dunaway. In Washington, it was Diron Talbert, Sonny Jurgensen, Billy Kilmer, Jack Pardee, Len Hauss, and Jake Scott.

Paul Maguire was probably the funniest of my dad's teammates. Diron Talbert was a riot, too. We were living in Reston and the upcoming game was against the Cowboys. Diron was over and one of our neighbor kids, David, was over, an obnoxious little kid about nine or ten. He came over in his Dallas Cowboys PJs and started taunting Diron: "Cowboys are going to win! Cowboys are going to win!" Diron opened the front door and tossed him out and shut the door! Mom said, "Now, Diron, you can't be throwing the neighbor kids around."

He played from the day I was born until I was eighteen. I sometimes wonder what my life would have been like if my dad hadn't gone to Buffalo. He was cut from Minnesota, packed the family up (at the time just Taz and I), and moved back to Toledo, fully expecting to become a junior or senior high school industrial arts teacher. Mom was a PE teacher. I would have had a completely different life.

Dad influenced what I wanted to do with my life. I got a degree in sports broadcasting and worked in radio and TV. I got my love of sports from both my parents (Mom was an Olympic contender diver and got a full diving scholarship to the Purdue *men's* diving team). I was taught a strong work ethic, humor, storytelling, and honesty.

Taz's Story

Taz McDole is my oldest son, and he also jotted down a few memories for the book: "Growing up with Ron McDole as your dad was both exciting and daunting. I remember going to the games and walking out of the stadium tunnel carrying his bags, and being so damn proud when we hit the crowd waiting at RFK. Everyone was waiting there, wanting his autograph. I also remember how scared I was when I started playing football. Coaches thought I was going to be great because my dad was still playing. I was great in my mind playing *Monday Night Football* up on the lighted tennis courts at Hook Road in Reston with my buddies.

"A lot of my memories are of Ron McDole, the woodworking guy, not Ron McDole, the football guy. Dad was a hard worker, and he made sure that we learned what hard work would get you. My sister Tammy and I had to move two pallets of building bricks every spring while we built our house. We'd move them 20 yards away from the house, and then back the following year. We did this until we moved out of Eden, New York. I went to work in his woodworking shop when I was eleven. We always did our own remodeling.

"I never looked at his fame as an opportunity. I always referred to it as his job. I am a lot like Ron; he really never talks about his days in the AFL and the NFL unless you ask him about it. I also don't tell people about Dad unless asked. I am very proud of him and his accomplishments. But his football career isn't what defines him at all. Today, I'm a master cabinet builder because of what he taught me. I also own an investment company. He taught me how to work hard and treat people with kindness and respect."

Appendix 1

Interview with Pat Fischer

Pat Fischer was my Nebraska teammate. We both were drafted by the St. Louis Cardinals in 1961 and we later became NFL teammates when I joined the Redskins. In November 2016, we sat down and talked about our parallel careers.

Pat: I cannot remember the very first time I met you, but obviously, it had to be at the University of Nebraska, and it was probably in the dining area. At Nebraska, there was a special little dining area just for the athletes on scholarships; it was in the back section of the dining room. That's where we would have breakfast, lunch, and dinner; all three meals were provided. The football team would also have meetings in the dining room occasionally, as well as meetings above the basketball coliseum and at the football stadium. They were always prepared and they would have books, paper, and diagrams and drawings for the offense and defense.

We had summer jobs at college, too. I went and worked in the oil rigs. I also got paid to go dig up bones. Did you dig up bones? You could make nine bucks digging up bones.

Ron: No. I did not do that. You did.

Pat: Yeah. I did that.

Ron: We also taught driver's education in the summers.

Pat: Oh, yeah! Driver's education. We didn't even wreck the car, and we got college credit for teaching it. You know, we did what we had to stay eligible to play in college. That was tough, going to summer school. How did you make it through ROTC? Remember, we had two years of that. We had to march around. You never showed up! Ron, you didn't even have a uniform!

Ron: You know what we used to do? We had to wear those uniforms for parades, and we had parade every Thursday of the year. So, to get out of it, we'd tape our arms and limp and act like we were hurt so we didn't have to do it. Those were tough times. We were there during the Berlin Crisis. We dodged that bullet.

Pat: We lost some of our players to that. I would have gone into the air force.

Ron: Someone told me that you were in the air force. I thought, "Pat, in the air force? Shit, he can't even see!"

Pat: I ended up down at Lackland Air Force Base in Texas. Eight weeks of basic training. They made me the PT instructor. The toughest part was standing up on that big stand in front of everybody, yelling, "Start running! Keep going!"

Ron: You know, it's funny. I was just thinking about when Pat and I met for the first time at Nebraska. I thought Pat was a quarterback or something. I didn't know anything about him. And as we got to know each other, I found out that there is a whole House of Fischers! There are tons of Fischers, and they are all superb athletes. I found out you had all these sisters, and they were all great athletes. Everywhere I went in Nebraska, people would talk about the Fischers, and what a great family they were, and how many great athletes they had, and how many had played at Nebraska! So, I heard there was a Fisher on the football team, I wanted to know more about this great athlete. But when I looked around for him he was hurt or something.

Pat: Yeah, they had this training program and I got mono. I also got hit in the head or something.

Ron: So when I finally see Pat Fischer for the first time, it was when the team was assigning rooms and roommates. Somebody pointed him out to me and I thought, "Hell, he is *really small!*" But heck, I'm a believer in anything, and I was then, too. So, what the hell. But early in the season, he was hurt or something and he wasn't around much. I think he ended up missing his first season.

Pat: Yes, I did. My freshman year, I only played in two games—against Kansas and Missouri.

Ron: Pat comes back from his illness, and we're all thinking, "Right, well, he better be good!" And Pat takes the opening kick-off for a touchdown! We were all screaming and yelling. This guy was fantastic! My God, who would have thought this little runt can play football! I remember we lined up and you were the only guy in Nebraska history that has ever been a double quarterback. We had a two-quarterback formation. It was illegal as hell, but we did it.

Pat: That we did! We lined up two guys in the position to receive the ball from the center—Tom Kramer and me. And we'd stand there to receive the ball. One of us would run one way and the other would run the other way, and the fullback would come up and we would fake to him and no one knew where the hell the ball was! We did two or three plays until the officials stopped us and said it was illegal.

Ron: Another thing, Pat. Most people these days do not realize that in those days, we players played both ways—offense and defense. We played all the time on both.

Pat: Yes, we did. We had to. If a player was on the field, he could only go off and come back in one time every quarter. So, we *had* to play both ways.

Ron: Pat was a smoker. He smoked those damn cigarettes all the time—*all* the time. Students were not allowed to smoke on campus, at least not the ball players. When Pat and I became the team captains, we saw each other all the time. I would see him cutting across the campus, smoking, trying to get off campus. It didn't bother me any. Our head coach, Jennings, called me to his office one afternoon. I had no idea what for. So, I go over to the athletic office and there's Jennings, along with some of the other coaches, and I ask, "What's up?"

Jennings says, "You know Fischer smokes all the time?" "Well, yeah, I know," I say. "And you know he's not supposed to smoke?" he asks. "I know that," I say.

"Fischer is going to be a team captain. What do you think we should do about his smoking habit?" "I don't know. Do you coaches see him smoking often?" I ask.

"Well, yeah," says Jennings. "Whenever we go to lunch we see him smoking while he's walking on campus, or smoking while walking across the street." I say, "Well, I can tell you this. He's not going to stop smoking." He says, "Yeah. That's what we feel about it, too. But we need to make a decision."

"Maybe if we don't cut across campus, we won't see him smoking," I suggested. "Hmm. Okay," Jennings says. And as far as I know, they never did anything about it.

Pat: You know, back in college, we were expected to go to church. The campus Catholic Church was called the Newman Center. A lot of the football players would go on Sundays, and we used to sit in the back row.

Ron: Pat and I ran around together, like we do now, and I used to stay at his house and his mother would make us go to church.

Pat: Well, we would head out the door, and at least *pretend* to be heading to church.

Ron: Yup. We had certain rules, and going to church was one of them. It didn't matter what religion you were. You could even be an atheist, if you went to church on Sunday. Paula was Catholic. For us to get married, we both had to be Catholic, so I decided to join the Catholic church. And I asked Pat to be my godfather.

Pat: That's right. I'm Ron's godfather.

Ron: We were sitting in the student union in Nebraska after Pat and I learned that we'd both been drafted by the now–St. Louis Cardinals. We had no idea what was going to happen. We both knew we had to stay at least one more semester to get our university degree, and I remember talking with you about it and wondering whether we should go for it or not. Did we really want to do this? We sat there in the booth at the student union for a long time, thinking about it, discussing the pros and cons about whether we should do it or not, and we came to the same conclusion. Let's go do it! If we don't go try to play professional football, then we'll never know whether we could have made it or not. And if we do go to training camp, at least we can tell our kids about it, whether we make it or not.

Now, all we needed was a ride to training camp. We all packed into that damn tiny little Fiat with the sunroof. Paula and I sat in the front seat—we were married and had our daughter Tammy by now—and you, Pat, sat in the back seat with Tammy. She was in a basket, but she had colic, and she started crying, so you had to hold her and bounce her most of the way to Michigan for training camp. Tammy cried most of the time. It seemed like we were never going to get there. And then finally, we get closer to the big city, and poor Pat had never seen anything like it, having lived in Nebraska your whole life. You kept saying, "Look at the roads! They have four lanes going each direction!" You'd never seen eight lanes of traffic before. "Look at all these people! All these cars! Oh, my God, look at all that water!" We were driving by Lake Michigan.

As we got closer to training camp, the road became a normal two-lane road again, and we drove north, all the way up to our first training camp. Man, that was different. All these famous guys were there, guys we'd read about or heard about.

Pat: Yes. Guys like Bobby Joe Conrad, Sonny Randle, Sam Estebury, John David Crow.

Ron: You see, the Cardinals had a lot of older players. They were the old Bears, and the team and the players had been around forever. Most of the guys at training camp that were already on the Cardinals were *a lot* older than we were. I had been drafted by St. Louis in the fourth round, because the Cardinals were looking for someone to replace Frank Ford. Ford had told the team that he was going to retire. He lived out in California, and he didn't want to play anymore. I'm thinking, well, maybe I have a job if I can win Ford's former position. I kept praying that he would not come back to training camp. But he did come back! So, I had to go play a different position.

Pat: They had a lot of old players. Bobby Joe and Taz Anderson were there, too, right?

Ron: Yeah. Some of the guys got out of having to sing the school song at hazing. You never had to do it. I think they were just afraid of you!

Pat: No, I think they thought I was there as the equipment manager. They didn't know I was there to make the team.

Ron: Pat, you and I were like Mutt and Jeff. You were real small and I was big, and the big thing was that we had showed up to training camp together and we made an odd pair. They looked at us and you could hear them thinking, "Well, the big guy looks like he can play ball, but what the hell does this other guy do!?"

Pat: Remember, the Cardinals didn't even have any equipment that would fit me, so I didn't practice. I can't remember how long that lasted, but I just sat on the sideline.

Ron: Yes. The Cardinals didn't know what to do with you. They tried you as a receiver. They had no idea you couldn't see, and there you were out there trying to catch balls that you couldn't see!

Pat: I was the punt returner for that first game against Canada. . . . Wasn't that the first game we played? We went up to Toronto.

Ron: That was the most difficult part of training camp that first year: sweating it out, worrying about getting cut. We'd never had to worry about that before.

Pat: Yeah. Go hide! "The coach wants to see you, and bring your playbook." Those were the words you did not want to hear!

Ron: I'll never forget when we got our first paycheck as rookies in St. Louis after we made the team. Pat was single and I was married and had a family. I could not wait to get my first check. It was not a lot of money, but I had $500 extra in my paycheck. I asked what this was about and they said if you made the team you got a $500 bonus! I said, "That's fantastic, thank you!" I hauled back to where we were staying and I was excited. We all lived in the bird house area . . .

Pat: That's right. Every street was named after a bird.

Ron: I was a bird lover, so that made me happy! Pat was staying with Giuliani and Martin Shy the bartender and another guy. I said, "Fischer, we got an extra $500, isn't that fantastic?"

Pat said, "What 500 bucks?" I asked, "Didn't you get your paycheck?" He said, "Heck, no. I haven't picked up my paycheck in 3 weeks!" "Oh, my God," I said. "It must be nice that you don't even have to worry about getting paid! Here I am trying to support a family, and you haven't even picked up your paycheck!" But Pat ran down there and got his paycheck with that big $500 bonus for making the team.

Ron: So, Pat, I played only one season on the Cardinals. You were there a long time. When did you finally leave the Cardinals?

Pat: After ten years I played out my option. I wanted more money, and they were not going to give it to me. I knew that in advance. Someone from the Redskins contacted me when they heard that I was playing out my option, so I knew if I played it out I was going to have a job in Washington. At the time, I thought the Redskins were giving me a $1,500 bonus, but it ended up being an advance on my contract, assuming I made the team. I didn't know this, so after I played and got my first paycheck, I did the math and realized something was wrong. That's when I learned it was an advance and not a bonus.

Ron: Everyone thinks that the NFL is so pure and doesn't do anything wrong, and in reality, what they did—and what they do—to guys is unbelievable. Yeah, you're all right, you're fine, you're healthy. Now run down to the 30-yard line. You do what they say and then they cut you anyway. Pat, what was Sonny Randle like when you played with him in St. Louis?

Pat: He was the head Cardinal. He never talked to me.

Ron: The only reason he ever talked to me was because of this dance class. Paula wanted to take this dance class, and Sonny was in that class. So was Frank Fuller. Some of the weirdest guys were in that dance class. Their wives made them get in the damn class. Pat did not have a wife, so no dance class for him.

Pat: Yeah. You know, I can't think of many funny stories from St. Louis. Well, I made the team. That was funny.

Ron: One funny story, Pat. I heard that Joe Theismann was your roommate later in your career?

Pat: Yes. Joe Theismann and I were roommates on away games and one year for training camp.

Pat: I remember one year, we were on the train going to a game against the Philadelphia Eagles. You and I were in the back with all the players, and you had a card game going on over there, and Sam Wyche was doing his magic tricks, which was really fascinating, and we were collecting everyone's twenty dollars to put down a bet on a horse race. Tommy McVean got a guy with a car to go to place the bet. The equipment guy on the Eagles was going to put all his money on this race. We were trying to get our bets in in time, and I'm collecting money for the bets.

Ron: George Allen is having Pat study, and everyone is having a good time playing cards or watching the magic. The bet on the race, which is a huge long shot, is soon forgotten. We get to Philly and found out that the bets were placed and we all made eighty dollars off of our twenty dollars of lunch money. That was a big deal, because at the time that was big money, because a lot of the guys did not game and everyone now had a few extra dollars in their pockets. We played the game in Philadelphia, and we almost got beat. Eddie Brown was in the game near the end for the Redskins, and the Eagles were working their way down the field. Eddie got a great interception and we won. After the game, we were in the locker room and everyone was rah rah rah because we won. George was saying that we have to give the game ball away. He asked all of us, "Who should I give the game ball to?" Everyone says, "Pat Fischer!" George was confused as to why Pat, but he gave the ball to Pat.

Pat: I got the game ball because the horse won! I didn't do anything in the game, but the horse won!

Ron: George never knew why everyone nominated Pat until later when we were at a sports banquet. Everyone was saying a few words about everyone, and Pat gets up and says, "George, I really did not win that game ball for the game. But I collected everybody's money for the horse race and it won."

Ron: Pat, what do you think is the reason that you and Mick Tingelhoff and I managed to have such long careers?

Pat: I wish I knew the answer to that. That would be something that we could share with our children. There are things you could teach to help prevent injury. I guess that is the answer. And, really, if you want to do something bad enough you can achieve it.

Ron: Yeah. But also, if you think back about it, and I have thought about it many times. . . . With me, it was the migraines. I look back now and I think about how those almost put me out of football. There are lots of things that can shorten your career. So, I try to think what I did differently than anyone else. And I think about how people have told me, "You were running all the time. You ran all over the field. You run to the left side of the field to make plays, and then you run to the right. You're never standing around." And then there's the fact that I insisted on always wearing a two-bar facemask. I wore a two-bar mask because I wanted to see. Maybe that kept me from getting hurt.

Pat: I think you wore the two-bar because you wanted to get an interception!

Ron: Oh, yeah, I always wanted an interception! I want to see the ball, I wanted to place the ball. When I put the cage on it caged me in and I could not see. I think another reason I managed to play eighteen years in the pros was that I've never really been sick, never had any childhood diseases.

Pat: You never got hurt! How many games did you miss because of injury?

Ron: None. Well, no. I missed one game in 240 games.

Pat: I played in 213 games, and I never missed any games, either, until right at the end of my career.

Ron: So how did you escape getting hurt?

Pat: Well, I didn't want to admit to any injury and didn't want to report any injury. I just took care of it on my own because I didn't want the trainer or anyone else to know about it.

Ron: Ed Henke told me this: "The one place you do not want to be is in the training room! Never, never go to the training room unless someone has to carry you there, because once you go in there you get the rep." Another thing that I think is true, too: I never lay on the field. I had to be knocked to the field.

Pat: Me neither.

Ron: Remember George Saimes on the Bills? He's passed away now, but he was a great safety for us with Buffalo—he took hits and licks. Some of them looked like they should have killed him. But George would never come off the field, and the only way you would ever see him come off the field is if they had to carry him off. He never did come off the field for an injury. My biggest problem was that I was afraid of my head—that if I got my head hit again that then the migraines would come back and my career would be over. They knew about my head injury. I got cold-cocked a few times in games, but there was no way I was laying on that field. I had to get back up and keep going, because if not, they would have me back on the way to that damned hospital.

Pat: Ice. Lots of ice. Then get in the whirlpool. Lots and lots of ice. Football really has changed a lot over years, though. I had older brothers who played football, and one was a high school coach, and there was always lots of tackling and rehearsing, running drills over and over. My brother Kenny would set up three dummies and everyone had to run through them with the football and you had to try to tackle them. Learning how to tackle and not being afraid to tackle is the most important part of becoming a good football player. Learning that there was not any danger if you did it right, and you were not going to get hurt. In fact, if you know how to tackle, then the more aggressive you were the better off things were going to be. I guess you can get hurt, and I have had some injuries. But over the years, the player that is active and aggressive is the dominant player.

Ron: Players don't know how to tackle anymore. They do not spend the time. Instead, they spend their time building up their bodies, which is necessary, but they do not spend the time training the bodies they build. I'll give you a great example. My entire career, everyone told me that you have to lift weights to be successful in the AFL or the NFL. I said, "I don't like lifting weights—I lift enough weight lifting my body!" I don't mind doing barbell exercises, light exercise for motion. "Here is my thought about lifting weights," I would tell everybody. "I'm more worried to get from this point to that point to make the tackle, than to stand there and see whether I could out-lift this guy." I always felt that if I could run and move and hustle then I'd be fine. I played handball and racquetball, which was excellent training for what I did on the field—much better than lifting a weight. A youth coach wrote me a letter one time asking me what I would recommend his kids do to train. I told him to get them playing handball or racquetball or out on a tennis court. In any of those sports, you have to go right, left, frontward, or backward as fast as you can.

Ron: What do you think about the lawsuit on concussions?

Pat: I am part of that lawsuit, so I appreciate it. It is tough for ball players. I experienced it. The lawsuit is an ongoing thing. It hasn't been settled and I do not think it will ever be settled.

Ron: I do not think it is ever going to happen, because the insurance companies who are involved are going to have to pay the money, so they are also going to sue.

Pat: It's been going on for three years. Sadly, in another ten years, everyone who needs it, and anyone it really helps, will be dead.

Ron: The sad thing about it is that everyone thinks we are going to make lots of money from this. We do not get a dime. They would take care of us if we get sick, but that's it. The people who really got screwed were all the players older than us. Those men don't get anything. Guys like Johnny Unitas. They're just waiting for all the old guys to all die, and then they don't have to worry about it. And it's the same thing with us. They're just waiting for us to be gone, too.

Ron: So what do you think has kept you and me friends for fifty-plus years?

Pat: You're making the assumption that we *are* friends. [Laughter from both parties] Gosh, how many times have we been guest speakers together? We've traveled many, many miles together. I always let you drive, Ron, because you're the superior driver and you stay awake. We've also gone to the Hall of Fame inductions three times—for Coach George Allen, for Chris Hanburger, and for Mick Tingelhoff. Ron, you've been my good friend for many, many years. And you always will be.

Appendix 2

McDole's Annual and Career Stats

Roland Owen McDole (Nickname: "The Dancing Bear")

Position: DE-DT

6 feet 4 inches, 265 lbs. (193 cm, 120 kg)

Born: September 9, 1939, Chester, Ohio, USA

College: University of Nebraska

NFL Draft: 1961 / Round 4 / Pick 50, St. Louis Cardinals

AFL Draft: 1961 / Round 4 / Pick 25, Denver Broncos

Jersey numbers worn: 66, 84, 72, 79

Teams played for: St. Louis Cardinals (1961), Houston Oilers (1962), Minnesota Vikings (1962), Buffalo Bills (1963–69 in AFL, 1970 in NFL), Washington Redskins (1971–78)

Regular season games played: 240

Total games played: 251

Career stats:

	Games	INTS	TDS	Yards	Long	Fumble Rec	Yds	TDS	Safeties
Regular season	240	12	1	115	42	14	25	1	3
Postseason	11					1			
Total	251	12	1	115	42	15	25	1	3

Awards won:

American Football League 2nd Team All-1960s Team

American Football League All-Pro Team (1964, 1966)

Interceptions by a lineman: 12 (NFL record)

Career safeties: 3 (fourth all-time)

Top 70 Redskins of All Time

AFL Championship Team: 1964–1965

Super Bowl: VII (1972)

Index